Magic of WATERCOLORS

by Tom Lynch

This book is based on the television series *Magic of Watercolors*, produced by KOCE-TV, Huntington Beach, California. Production of the television series was made possible by a grant from

KOCE-TV FOUNDATION
HUNTINGTON BEACH, CALIFORNIA

MAGIC OF WATERCOLORS
KOCE-TV Foundation
P.O. Box 2729
Huntington Beach, California 92647

BOOK STAFF

Executive Editor
Valerie Lynch Lee

Editor
Mary Lou Ferrante

Production Manager
Gene Booth

Cover Design
Carl Glassford

Photography
Nrapendra Prasad
Valerie Avellar

Printed in the United States of America

First Printing, 1984

FROM TOM LYNCH

If you have an open mind and a positive attitude about painting, the pages ahead will be easy and fun for you.

Part of the confidence in yourself and in your work will develop even *before* you begin to paint if you allow yourself time to be an artist, time to get in the mood of your painting, time to plan, sketch, and practice.

If you're going to be an artist, you have to have a place where you can paint and study your work, where you can leave things the way they are and, when you come back, pick up things where you left them. It can be a corner but it should be *yours*, off limits to others, away from distractions. Even if you don't paint at that moment, you're helping your creative process by encouraging your imagination and mood.

But when you do paint, you'll need paints, brushes, paper, and other supplies. These special materials are explained in the first section of this book, and I encourage you to read it carefully, especially if you haven't painted with watercolors before. As you read this section, remember the one special ingredient you need—and it's free—is *enthusiasm*. Without it, you really can't paint. My favorite paintings come from my heart, so put a smile on your face, be determined, think positively, and then charge ahead!

The second section of this book, Watercolor Painting Techniques, is even more critical because you must know and understand how to use those materials and supplies before you can really concentrate on being an artist and creating a painting.

In this section, I encourage you to practice many different techniques with your paints and brushes. As you practice, these techniques will soon become fun as you gain control of them (instead of their controlling you) and learn about all the wonderful effects you can achieve with your watercolor paints and brushes. And the results of your practice needn't go to waste. If you produce something you like on your paper, trim the edges neatly and frame it or use it as a note card or greeting card.

When I paint, I spend a lot of time getting myself

in the mood to paint. I look at photographs and pictures I've saved and sketches I've made that recall for me the feeling I want to capture on paper. If I'm going to paint a casual picture, I get comfortable in my studio with slippers, a fire in the fireplace (in the winter), a cup of tea, music.

After you set the mood, planning is the next step. I love the research and plotting out that each picture requires—thinking about the scene I want to paint, where I want my center of interest to be, and how I'm going to paint each part. If I'm not sure about the colors, I'll spend time mixing them on the palette, mentally looking at a variety of colors.

This planning just naturally gets me sketching and practicing strokes and techniques. A sketch is not copying the details of a scene for you to paint. It's an aid to *creating* a painting. And since watercolor painting is a fast medium, it necessitates a practice stage. Here, the mistakes won't matter. With practice, mistakes or what I consider weaknesses will become strengths. Every effort you make, the planning and practice, will be of value to you.

Like magic, all the time you spend getting ready to paint makes you so confident and eager to actually begin that any fears or uncertainties you had disappear! Watercolor is the best medium for painting moods and feelings. It doesn't take twenty years' experience to do the paintings in this book. In fact, some of the paintings are relatively easy for a first-time painter.

When you do the paintings in this book, you'll learn the fundamentals—how colors set a mood or give a sense of time, how values of light and dark create drama and depth, what characterizes interesting shapes, and how to make hard and soft edges. With each new painting, you'll reinforce the techniques you've used to dramatize the effects you want. As you paint, you'll see that painting every detail is really not important, that making mistakes is OK, and that you can loosen up and make more natural-looking paintings.

Once you've read the first two introductory sections, you're off to a good start. I know you can achieve in your own paintings what I have done in mine.

Throughout this book and the television series, my goal has been to introduce you to the fun and excitement of painting in watercolor. My hope is that, as you paint, you'll expand your talent, possibly even taking classes in advanced watercolor techniques. I know that you never stop learning with watercolors. I still consider myself a student intent on becoming a master.

I know there is not *one* way to paint. I have been taught by some of this country's master watercolorists, people like John Pike, Ed Whitney, Robert E. Wood, Zoltan Szabo, Nita Engle, Irving Shapiro, and others. I am a product of all my instructors. There are touches of each of them in what I do. Expanding someone else's idea or applying someone else's technique is my way of passing it on to you.

Tom Lynch

This book is dedicated to all those who have a dream and who, through hard work, determination, and positive thinking, have achieved that dream.

This one is for you, Tami, so your wish will come true as well.

CONTENTS

INTRODUCTION

- *Paints, Brushes, Paper and Other Supplies for Watercolor Painting*
- *Watercolor Painting Techniques*

PAINTS, BRUSHES, PAPER, AND OTHER SUPPLIES FOR WATERCOLOR PAINTING

The purpose of this section is to acquaint you with all the basic materials, tools, and supplies you'll need for the watercolor paintings in this book and, indeed, for almost any watercolor painting.

Please read this section carefully because the information it contains about paints and brushes, type of watercolor paper to use and how to prepare it, and the other supplies is really critical to the successful creation of a watercolor painting.

Also, this information provides a foundation for the next section of this book, Watercolor Painting Techniques, in which you will learn about how to use paints, brushes, and other supplies in both basic and specialized watercolor techniques.

PAINTS

Watercolor paintings have their freshness and brilliance because watercolor paints, although they appear opaque as they come out of the tube, become transparent once they are mixed with water. The transparency then lets the whiteness of the paper show through.

For the paintings in this book—and for all my painting—I use tube watercolors (Speedball brand). I recommend that you also use tube watercolors and that you buy good quality paints with pure, bright pigments, not dulled with fillers. Also, squeeze out fresh paint every day you paint; don't try to save your paint overnight.

For all the paintings in this book, you'll need only nine different colors:

- Lemon Yellow
- Yellow Ochre
- Speedball Red
- Permanent Magenta
- Cerulean Blue
- Cobalt Blue
- Ultra Blue
- Payne's Gray
- Burnt Sienna

Notice that there are only two yellows—a light (Lemon Yellow) and a dark (Yellow Ochre) and two reds—a bright light red (Speedball Red) and a dark, bluish red (Permanent Magenta).

There are three blues—a light (Cerulean), medium (Cobalt), and a dark (Ultra).

Payne's Gray is a black paint with a fair amount of blue in it. I use it to darken other colors and, mixed with Lemon Yellow, to make a deep green. Burnt Sienna is a rich reddish brown that I use to add deep warm tones to paintings.

If you have never painted with watercolor paints before, but have painted with oils or acrylics, you may wonder about the absence of white. In watercolor, water, not white paint, is used to lighten paint. And, for objects that are pure white, that part of the paper is simply not painted.

To do watercolor paintings you really don't need any more than the nine colors listed above. These colors can be mixed with each other and diluted with water to create countless numbers of other colors and shades, and I urge you to learn about those colors and shades by practicing and experimenting with your watercolor paints.

PALETTE

To hold your paints while you paint, you'll need a palette. Palettes for watercolor paints come in many styles. The palette you use should have a sufficient number of small wells to hold all the colors you'll be using, as well as a very large central well in which to mix several different colors with water. The palette should also have a lid, so that if you have to stop painting for a short while, you can place a damp sponge in the center well, and then put on the lid to keep your paints moist.

Tubes of the nine different watercolor paints used for the paintings in this book.

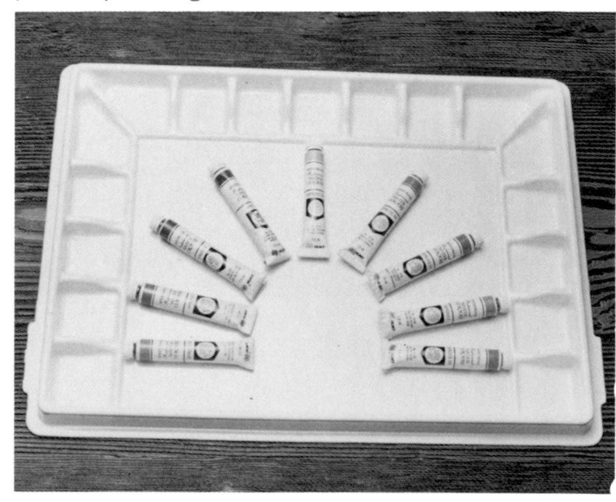

The four most frequently used brushes for watercolor painting. From the left: 1-inch flat wash watercolor brush, ½-inch flat wash watercolor brush, No. 7 round wash watercolor brush, No. 4 fine-point round watercolor brush.

BRUSHES

Brushes are the tools with which you apply watercolor paints to paper to create your painting. As with your paints, quality is all important.

For the watercolor paintings in this book, you'll need four basic brushes: two flat wash watercolor brushes, one round wash watercolor brush, and one fine-point round watercolor brush. In addition, you may find several other brushes, such as a wide 2½-inch brush and lettering brushes useful for some of the paintings. Most of the flat and round brushes I use are manufactured by Raphaël.

Flat Wash Watercolor Brushes

Flat wash brushes are the most frequently used brushes for watercolor painting. They can be used to make many different brush strokes to produce a variety of effects.

These brushes have fairly long bristles and square corners. The ends of the bristles form a clean, sharp edge when wet.

Flat wash watercolor brushes come in many sizes, but only two are necessary for the paintings in this book: a No. 20, about 1-inch wide at the base, and a No. 12, about ½-inch wide at the base.

The bristles of flat wash brushes used for watercolor paint must be thick, to hold large amounts of paint, and they must also have excellent spring and bounce so that they return to their original straight shape after being pressed to the paper.

The flat wash brushes I use are made from pure red sable hair, which has excellent spring and bounce. These brushes are expensive, but you only need two. With proper use and thorough cleaning, they will last through several hundred paintings.

If you are just beginning to paint, you might try using synthetic white sable brushes made with nylon bristles. These brushes are considerably less expensive than pure red sable. Eventually, as you continue with watercolor painting, I think you'll want to invest in high-quality red sable brushes.

Incidentally, do not use brushes made of ox hair or camel hair. They simply do not have the right spring or bounce for watercolor painting.

Round Wash Watercolor Brush

The round wash watercolor brush is made from sable or squirrel hair and tapers to a point from a round, thick base. A round wash brush, because it is thick, holds a great amount of paint, so it is especially useful for quickly filling large areas of your painting with a single color.

The basic size of a round wash brush for the watercolor paintings in this book is a No. 7, with a diameter at the base of about ½ inch. You may find a slightly larger size, a No. 12, with a diameter of about 1 inch at the base, also helpful.

Fine-Point Round Watercolor Brush

This small round brush has fairly long bristles that taper to a fine point, which makes it invaluable for painting thin lines for branches and stems and for filling in small details in a landscape, such as animals and people.

The fine-point round brush I use is a No. 4, which is a versatile size. It is made of pure red sable, which produces smooth, clean, flowing lines.

Other Brushes

One brush you might also find useful in watercolor painting is a wide 2½-inch brush for quickly filling large areas of paper with paint of a single color.

Also, for painting very fine lines and other details,

you may want to use several lettering brushes, sometimes called "riggers." Two brushes that I use are a No. 6 pointed lettering brush and a No. 14 extra-long pointed lettering brush.

Regardless of the type of brush you are using, clean it thoroughly when you finish painting. Swirl the brush in water until all the paint is dissolved and then blot it dry. Lay the brush flat for storage. Do not store your brushes with the bristles pointing up because moisture can collect in the metal base.

PAPER

The paper on which you do your watercolor painting must be as good as your paints and brushes. For most of the paintings in this book and, indeed, for almost all watercolor painting, the paper to use is 140-pound cold-pressed, made from 100 percent rag fibers.

This paper is heavy enough to withstand some of the watercolor techniques such as scratching out and erasing paint, and it is thick enough so that you can use the other side if you do not like what you have painted on one side. "Cold-pressed" refers to a paper-finishing technique that makes the surface of the paper slightly textured, which helps, in turn, to add texture to some of your brush strokes. Also, the fiber content of the paper is important. Paper made of 100 percent rag fibers is acid free and will not become brittle or yellow over time.

Watercolor paper comes in a standard sheet size of 22-by-30 inches. For the paintings in this book, I used a half sheet (15-by-22 inches), a size that is comfortable for most people to use.

Watercolor paper of this weight must first be soaked, stretched, and dried before it is used to prevent the wet watercolor paints from causing the paper to buckle and become wavy.

To soak and stretch the paper, completely immerse a sheet cut to the size you will be using in water in a bathtub or a tray large enough to let the sheet lie flat. Let the sheet soak for about 30 minutes, lift it out of the water, let the surface water drain off, and then place the paper on a ⅜-inch thick sheet of fiberboard or plywood, cut slightly larger than the paper (an 18-by-24-inch size works well for a 15-by-22-inch sheet).

Center the wet sheet on the board and then, using a standard office stapler, opened flat to the "tack" position, staple one of the short ends to the board. The staples should be at least ¼-inch in from the edge of the paper. Be generous with your staples, using one about every inch. After stapling the ends, smooth and staple the top and bottom of the paper.

Staples can be removed with the point of a palette knife.

Once the paper is stretched and stapled to the board, let it dry. The paper must be completely dry before you paint on it, and this will probably take about 12 hours, possibly a few hours more or less depending on the temperature and humidity of the room in which the paper is drying.

To remove the staples after you have finished your painting, slide the point of your palette knife or the tip of a small screwdriver between the staple and the board and twist the point to lift up the staple.

Two of the paintings in this book—*Still Life* and *Autumn Walk*—were painted on different types of watercolor paper.

Still Life was painted on 100-pound illustration board (a sheet of watercolor paper fused to thick posterboard) because the lifting out of paint and rubbing with a towel called for in parts of this painting required a more durable surface.

Autumn Walk was painted on a sheet of 200-pound cold-pressed watercolor paper. This painting used a "wet-into-wet" technique that required that the entire sheet be very wet through a long first stage. This heavier-weight paper does not need to be soaked, stretched, and dried first, but for *Autumn Walk*, I soaked it in water for about 20 minutes so that all the fibers were completely saturated, and then started the painting. Because of the thickness of the paper, it stayed wet for a longer time than a lighter sheet.

Regardless of the type of paper on which you are painting, you should position your working surface so that the top of the paper is somewhat higher than the bottom, tilted at about a 15-degree angle. This slight slant helps colors to blend together. When you want to stop the blending, you will want the paper to be flat, so you should have a small block of wood or other object to slip under your painting to lift the bottom a few inches.

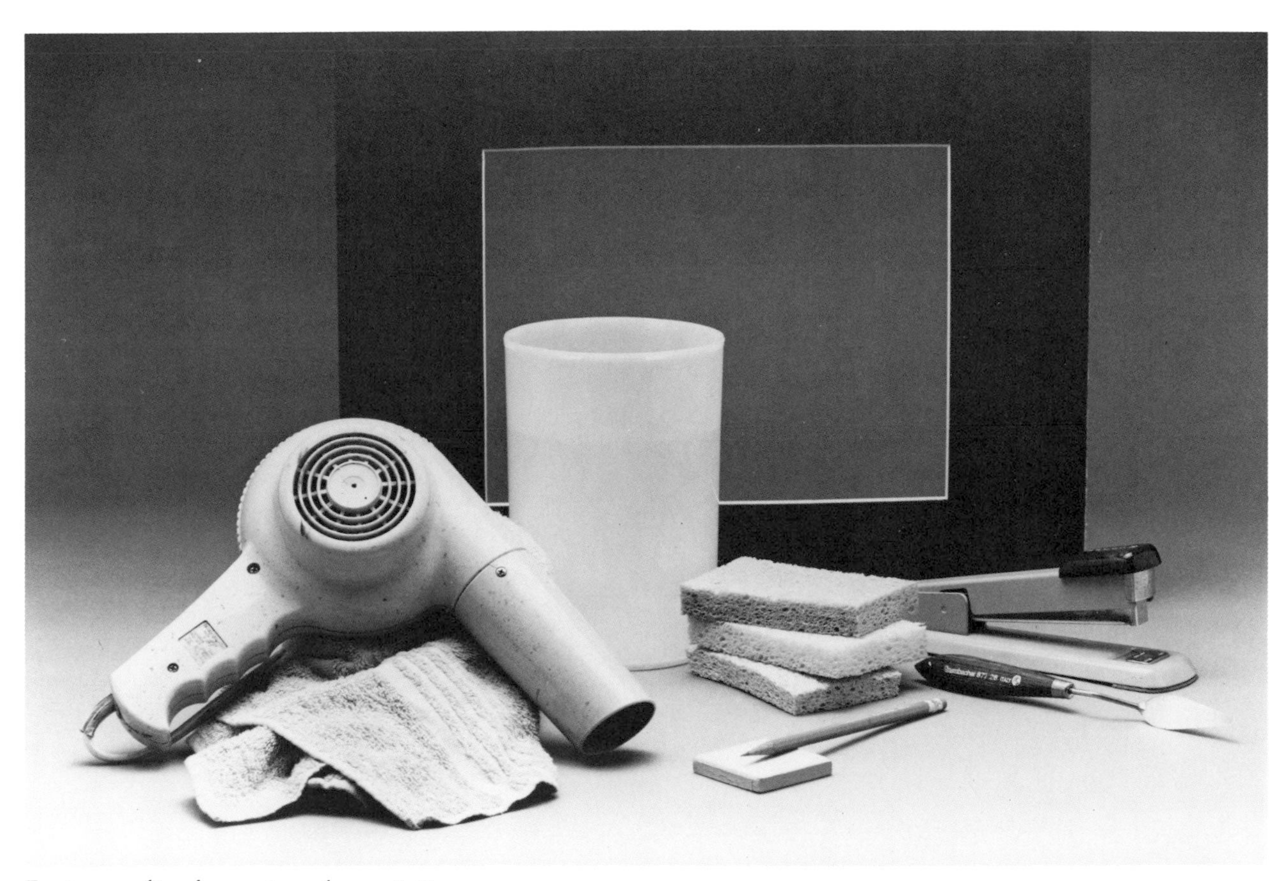

Basic supplies for watercolor painting.

OTHER SUPPLIES

In addition to paints, brushes, and paper, you'll need a few other basic supplies, as well as some special supplies to create various effects with watercolors.

Basic Supplies

One item every watercolor painter needs is a **water container.** The container can be a wide-mouthed glass jar, a plastic bucket, plastic food storage cannister, or almost anything as long as it is *large*.

The container should hold at least two quarts of water. You'll be dipping your brushes in the water frequently to clean them when you change colors as well as to add clean water to your palette. If you use a small container, the water will quickly become dirty, and you'll have to stop painting to empty and refill the container with clean water. So to save yourself trouble and to keep your colors bright and clear, please use a large container for your water.

You'll also need rectangular **household sponges.** You'll use the sponges to absorb excess water and paint from your brush and to clean out your palette when the paints have become muddied or when you want a clean area in which to mix a new color. It's important to have several sponges so that you'll always have a clean one.

Another useful item is a **terry towel** for quickly absorbing puddles of water and for blotting up water you have applied during several of the special watercolor techniques. For ease in handling, it should not be too large—a square about 18-by-18 inches should be about the right size. Also, it should be fairly thin so that you can easily crumple it to a small size for blotting a particular area.

For sketching before you begin to paint, you can use an ordinary **No. 2 writing pencil.** And for erasing any sketch lines, you should use a **kneaded rubber eraser,** which is very smooth and will not mar the surface of the watercolor paper.

I've already mentioned the need for an **office stapler** and a **palette knife** for stretching paper and then removing the staples after you have finished painting. You'll also use the point of the palette knife to scratch lines in wet paint.

Another very useful piece of equipment is a handheld **hair dryer.** Watercolor paintings are usually done in stages because it is necessary for one layer of paint to dry before painting over or next to it. Although the paint usually dries naturally in several minutes, depending on the wetness of the paper and the humidity of the room, a hair dryer can speed the drying time considerably.

If you do use a hair dryer, it is important to remember to hold it about 6 to 12 inches above the paper and to keep moving it around. If you hold it too close to the paper and over the same spot for too long, the force of the stream of hot air may push the wet paint around and form dark streaks and puddles.

However you dry your painting between stages, test to find out if it is dry by touching the paper with the back of your hand. If the paper feels cool, the paint is still wet and needs more drying. If the paper does not feel cool, the painting is sufficiently dry for the next stage.

Although not really needed for painting, I suggest that you buy several framing **mats,** cut to the size paper you most frequently use. Placing a mat around a painting when you are near to finishing it isolates it from surrounding clutter and lets you see how it will look when it is framed. You should have mats in various neutrals (white, ivory, beige, gray) as well as in several warm and cool colors to see how the different colors of mats add to—or detract from—a particular painting.

Special Supplies

The paintings in this book and most of the paintings I do require the use of a number of special supplies. With these supplies, you'll be able to create a wide range of wonderfully varied effects, beyond those that you can achieve with just paints and traditional watercolor brushes.

A **toothbrush** and a **cosmetic sponge** are two items that can be used to apply paint to create effects that cannot be achieved with traditional brushes.

By running your finger over a toothbrush loaded with paint, you can create a very fine spray of dots. I find it useful to have three toothbrushes, one for yellow, one for red, and one for blue, so that I don't have to clean them when I change colors.

With a cosmetic sponge, you can dab on paint to create an open, leafy effect in a very short time. The sponge is very useful for simulating the texture of leaves on a tree, for example. The sponge should be a *natural* one; synthetic sponges do not have the right texture. You can also use a damp cosmetic sponge to lift out paint from a small area.

Ordinary table **salt** is another supply that can be used to create some very special effects when sprinkled on wet paint.

I also use two kinds of bottles for spraying water—a **pump spray** and a **trigger spray.** The pump spray bottle is like that used for household window cleaning solutions. The trigger-spray bottle has an adjustable nozzle that can produce either a narrow, forceful stream or a wide, fine mist. By spraying water on wet paint you can create some additional blending and softening; by spraying on dry paint, you can remove some of the paint to lighten an area.

Cotton-tipped swabs can be used to rub out a narrow streak of paint, and **facial tissues** can be used to blot the edges of still-wet paint to soften them.

For completely removing dry paint to let the whiteness of the watercolor paper show in a finished painting, you can use a single-edge **razor blade** and an **electric eraser** or **ink eraser.**

A final group of special supplies includes items that can be used to protect the paper while you are painting, so that the area will remain white in the finished painting or so that you can add other colors in small areas in the final stages

Liquid frisket (Maskoid) is a gray masking material that can be painted over areas of your painting that you want to protect. Liquid frisket comes in a small jar, and you should apply it with an inexpensive small brush, such as an old **round brush** for better control. Immediately after applying liquid frisket, clean your brush with soap and water, lighter fluid, or turpentine.

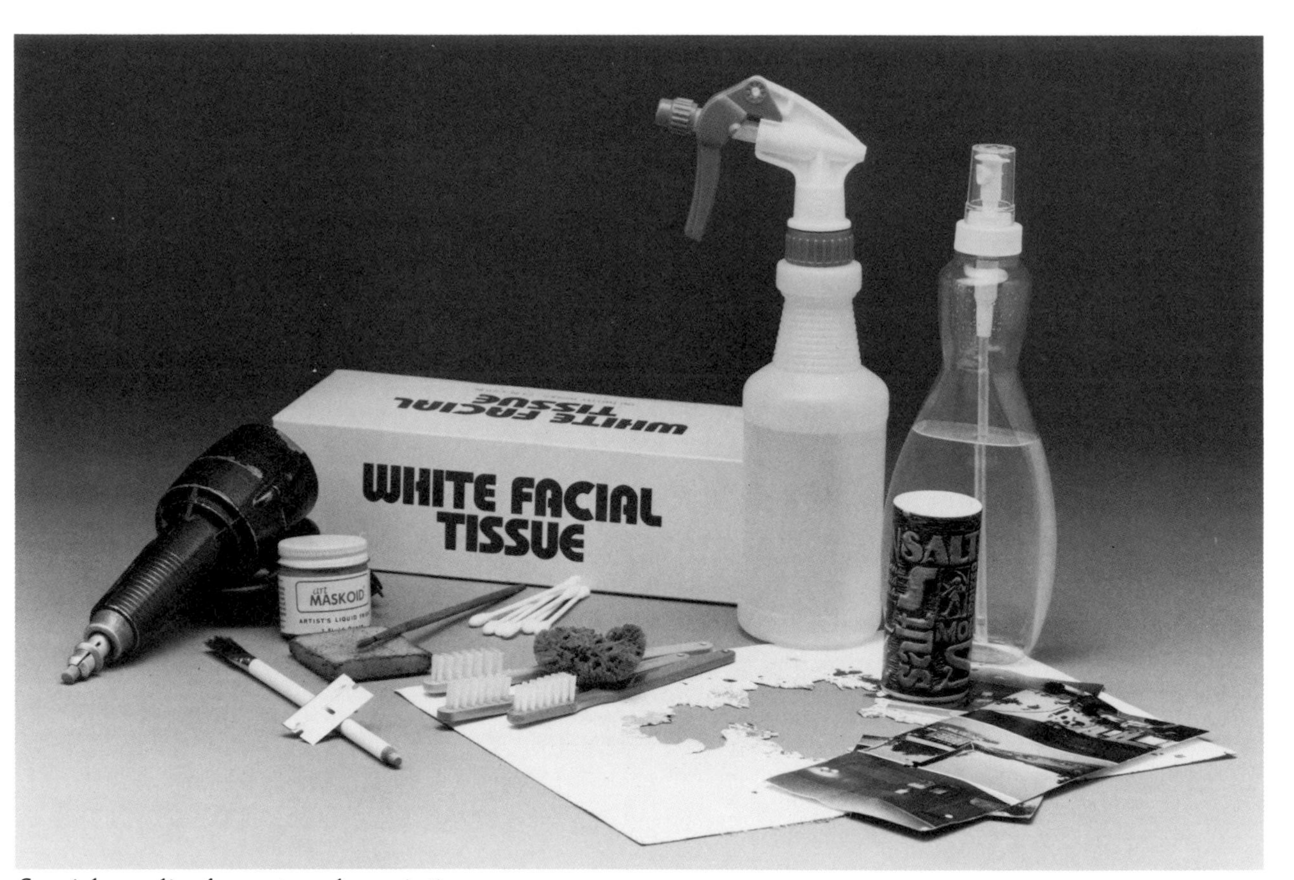

Special supplies for watercolor paintings.

To remove the liquid frisket after your painting is dry or when you are ready to paint in the area it has protected, you can either rub it off with your finger or with a **rubber cement pickup.**

Another way to protect paper when you're applying paint is to use a **stencil.** I make my stencils from stencil paper or a used sheet of watercolor paper. You can use the same or any material that is nonporous and will lie flat on your painting. To cut out the stencil, use scissors or an artist's knife, such as an X-Acto.

You may also want to protect paper when you remove paint from an already painted area to lighten it. If you want to have even, sharp edges where you remove the paint, you can use a **template.** I make my templates by taping postcards together. Postcards work well because the picture side is coated and repels water, so I do not have to worry about water soaking through to the area I am protecting.

Although it may seem that there are a lot of supplies for watercolor painting, they are really quite easy and enjoyable to use once you are familiar with them and with the variety of fascinating effects you can achieve.

The techniques for using these supplies are explained in the next section, Watercolor Painting Techniques, and I urge you to read it very carefully and to study the pictures closely, because that's where the "magic" of watercolors really begins.

WATERCOLOR PAINTING TECHNIQUES

For me, techniques are a means to an end, the end being the creation of a painting that expresses and captures a mood and my impression of a scene.

And in the creation of a painting I always strive to have *variety*. Variety contributes more to a painting than anything else. Variety is everything—variety of color, of value, of shape, of edge, of texture. And variety is what the techniques described on the following pages help me to achieve, and I hope they help you to achieve variety in your paintings.

For variety of color, I strive to have almost continuous color change throughout my paintings. Within those colors, I also have variety of values; that is, some colors are dark, some are medium, and others are light.

For variety of shapes, some objects are large; others are small; most are free form. And even on the edges of shapes I have variety. Some edges are sharp and crisp; others are irregular, ragged, or blurred. The spaces between shapes vary, too. Some spaces are wide, others are narrow.

For variety of texture, in some places I cover the paper completely and smoothly; in other places, I apply the paint brokenly. And after applying paint, I add further variety by breaking up the paint with dots of other colors, spraying drops of water, or sprinkling on salt.

I have developed and adapted these techniques to suit my own particular style of painting. I did not master them overnight, and in fact, almost every time I study and paint I discover some new way to create effects with watercolor paints.

I have learned these techniques by using them, and that's what I urge you to do. I believe in "learning by doing," so before you start a watercolor painting, please practice and experiment with these techniques. Mix paints with different amounts of water to learn about value. Mix different colors together to learn about making new colors. Experiment with loading your brush with different amounts of paint, and practice making brush strokes on dry paper, wet paper, and semi-dry paper. Sprinkle paint with salt and spray it with water. Splatter paint; let colors blend together. Above all, have fun with your watercolor techniques.

Don't let your techniques control you. Keep experimenting, testing, and trying out your paints, brushes, and other supplies with the techniques described here until you feel that you understand the range of effects you can achieve with watercolor painting and that *you* control those techniques. Once you have that understanding and control, start painting.

MIXING WATERCOLOR PAINTS AND WATER

The first thing to learn about watercolor techniques is how to mix watercolor paint and water.

As noted in the previous section on supplies, watercolor paint appears opaque when it comes out of the tube. Then, once it is mixed with water, it becomes transparent. The relative proportions of watercolor paint and water determine just how transparent and how light or dark the paint will be.

To mix watercolor paint and water, start with a clean palette and fresh paint. Take about a teaspoon of clean water by dipping your brush into water and then transferring the water in your wet brush to the palette, leaving a small puddle of water. Next, touch your brush to a sponge to absorb excess water, and then dip your brush into watercolor paint, move the loaded brush back to the water in the palette, and swirl the brush around in the water so that the paint in the brush is mixed in and diluted by the water. The resulting puddle of transparent watercolor is now ready to be applied to paper.

That's the basic technique for getting watercolor paint ready to apply. Of course, when you are actually painting, you will probably have more than one color in the central area of your palette, and your colors will probably be mixtures of two or more different colors rather than just one color.

Also, when you are painting, it is very important to mix your colors on the palette instead of on the paper because you have more control over the color on the palette than you have on the paper. Mixing your colors on the palette will also help you to avoid making streaks of pure paint on your paper.

Mixing and Value

The mixing of watercolor paints and water is fundamental to watercolor painting not only because it gets the paint ready to be applied but also because it is the relative proportions of paint and water that determine the lightness or darkness of a color and thus its **value.**

With a high proportion of water to paint, the color is very transparent and a light value; with a

Value *is determined by the relative proportions of water and paint. The top swatch has a high proportion of water and low proportion of paint and is of a light value. The two middle swatches have lower proportions of water to paint, and are of a medium value. The bottom swatch has a low proportion of water and a high proportion of paint and is of a dark value.*

low proportion of water to paint, the paint is barely transparent and a dark value.

The four color swatches at the bottom of the preceding page illustrate value. To make the swatches, I placed about a teaspoon of water in the center of a clean palette, touched a damp 1-inch flat watercolor brush to Cobalt Blue, swirled the brush in the water, and then stroked it across the paper to make the first, or lightest-value blue. For each succeeding (darker) swatch, I added more paint to the original puddle until, for the last, or darkest-value swatch, the proportion of paint to water was very high.

Try this exercise yourself, both with all the pure colors you use and with various mixtures of color. Also make more than four steps of values. It is certainly possible to have several shades lighter than the first one shown, as well as many intermediate values between the two middle values and the dark value.

APPLYING WATERCOLOR PAINTS

When you apply watercolor paints to paper, you will be trying to achieve a variety of effects with the paint. The effects you achieve are influenced by two factors: (1) the dryness or wetness of the surface and (2) the technique used to apply paint.

Dryness/Wetness of Surface

The surface to which watercolor paint is applied can be either dry or wet. The surface is dry if the paper itself is dry or if previously applied paint has dried. Painting on a dry surface is sometimes called "wet-on-dry." The surface is wet if the paper has been soaked or sprayed with water or if previously applied paint is still wet. Painting on a wet surface is called "wet-on-wet."

Paint applied to a dry surface will have sharply defined edges that will remain crisp, and the paint will be confined to the place it is applied. Paint applied to a wet surface will blur and blend and spread out.

The amount of blending and blurring depends on how wet the surface is. If the surface is very wet, the blending and blurring will be great. As the surface becomes less wet, the blurring and blending will diminish.

Most of the paintings in this book were painted on basically dry surfaces, although in certain areas of several paintings (*Summer Trees*, *Spring Sparkle*, *Iris*, and *Rustic Wagon*) I added some colors while earlier colors were still wet.

Three paintings in this book (*Autumn House*, *Harbor Sunrise*, and *Autumn Walk*) start with wet-on-wet technique but are finished with wet-on-dry technique.

Because both techniques are called for by the paintings in this book, it is especially important for you to understand how the dryness/wetness of a surface affects watercolor paints. To find out for yourself, wet a piece of watercolor paper and then apply paint to the paper over a period of five to ten minutes. The first stroke you make, when the paper is very wet, will blur greatly around the edges. But, as you make successive strokes as the paper dries, the blurring will lessen considerably until, when the surface is completely dry, the paint will not blur at all.

Two examples of graded washes.
The wash on top was done on dry paper.
The wash on bottom was done on wet paper.

Applying Paint with Brush Strokes

When paint is applied to paper with a brush, the area can be blocked in solidly with color or certain parts can remain unpainted, letting the white of the paper or colors applied earlier show through.

An area can be blocked in solidly with color with either a **flat wash** or a **graded wash.** In a **flat wash,** an area is filled with single color of the same value. In a **graded wash,** an area is filled with a single color that changes in value from top to bottom or from side to side. The illustration below shows graded washes on both wet paper and dry paper.

Practice both types of washes, using your 1-inch flat wash brush. As you apply each stroke, slightly overlap the top of the stroke over the bottom of the preceding stroke.

Several different types of strokes can be used to apply paint brokenly instead of solidly. The most frequently used of these strokes is called **drybrush.**

"Drybrush" is a somewhat misleading term because the brush is not really dry. In drybrush, the brush is actually damp, but dryer than it is when applying paint for a wash.

In drybrush technique, the brush is touched to a sponge after being loaded with paint. The sponge absorbs excess paint. When the brush is then stroked across the paper, the small amount of paint flows off the brush unevenly, leaving irregular, unpainted areas, an effect that is enhanced by the rough texture of the watercolor paper.

The amount of paint that flows off the brush is also affected by the speed of the stroke. A slow stroke will leave more paint than a fast stroke, as shown on the facing page.

As with flat washes and graded washes, practice and experiment with the drybrush technique on both wet and dry paper until you are confident of exactly how damp your brush should be and of how quickly or slowly you should move the brush to achieve various effects.

When the flat brush is used for washes and for drybrush strokes, the flat end of the brush is being moved across or down the paper and the bristles are bending slightly. However, many other basic strokes are made with the flat brush, using other parts and different motions. (See the illustrations on the facing page.)

The corner of the flat brush can be used to make

smooth horizontal lines. The thickness of the line varies with the amount of pressure applied as the brush moves across the paper. The corner of the brush can also be used to make short vertical strokes with a smooth downward motion.

Very fine straight lines can be made by holding the brush at a right angle to the paper and just touching the flat end to the paper.

The side of the brush can be used to scrape on paint to create a ragged, mottled effect. One scraping motion is made by placing the side of the brush against the paper and then turning it up. This stroke creates an area that is fairly solid with paint at the bottom and broken at the top. Another scraping motion is circular, with the side of the brush being moved across the paper in a series of continuous loops. This stroke creates an overall irregular effect.

Those are the basic techniques for stroking on paint with a brush and the ones that I have used for the paintings in this book. But numerous other special techniques are called for in these paintings. I used these techniques because they add even more variety and interest to my painting and enable me to take full advantage of the wonderful and unique characteristics of the medium of watercolor.

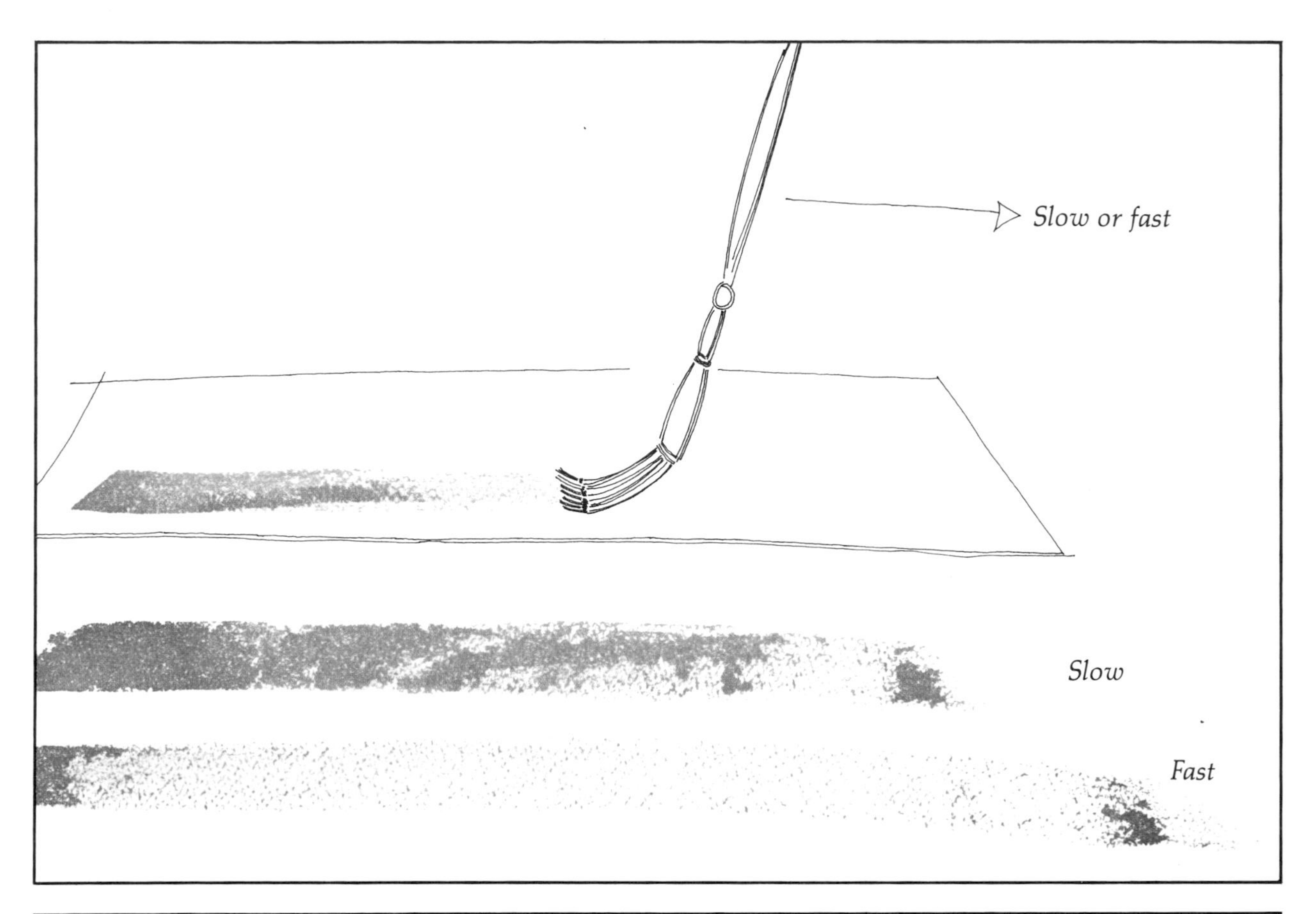

The effect produced by a drybrush stroke changes with the speed with which the stroke is made.

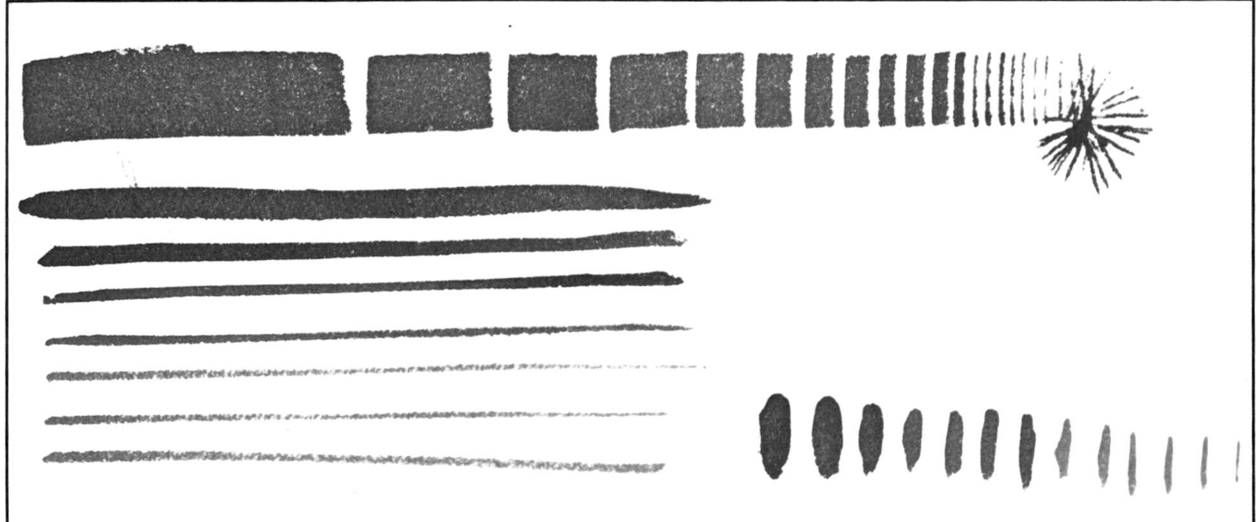

Many different strokes can be made with the flat brush. To make the brush strokes on the left in the top row, move the end of a flat brush, loaded with paint, smoothly across the paper. For the strokes at the right end of the row, hold the brush vertically to the paper and touch it lightly to the surface. To make the horizontal lines, use the corner of the flat brush; the amount of pressure determines their thickness. To make short vertical marks, also use the corner of the brush, pulling it down in short vertical strokes.

SPECIAL TECHNIQUES

Special techniques include applying paint by splattering with the flat brush and spraying on with a toothbrush; applying paint with a cosmetic sponge; sprinkling wet paint with salt; blending and softening colors; and lightening and removing colors.

Splattering

One technique I use frequently to apply paint is **splattering.** I like it because it adds freshness and crispness to a painting, and the results are always different.

To splatter, load your 1-inch flat wash brush (or ½-inch flat wash brush if you are splattering only a small area) with paint and hold the flat edge parallel to the paper. Raise the brush by bending your arm up at the elbow, lower your forearm smoothly, and then snap your wrist when your hand is over the paper (very similar to the way in which you shake down a thermometer). Different size dots of paint should fly off the bristles onto the paper (and often everywhere else). If the surface is dry, they will be fairly small; if the surface is wet, they will spread out and enlarge.

You can also splatter paint by tapping your brush against your finger. This technique is especially good if you want to confine the splattering to a relatively small area.

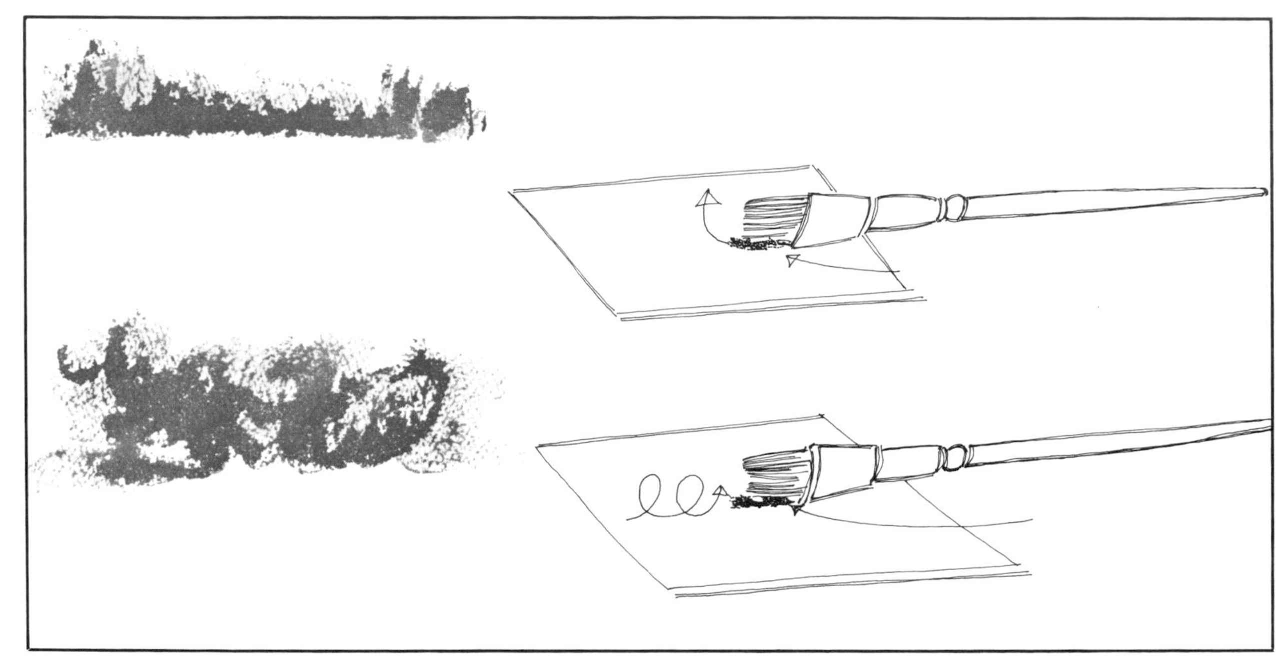

Two different scraping motions can be made with the side of the flat brush, and each produces a different effect. On the top, turn the side of the brush up and then lift it from the paper. On the bottom, scrape the brush in continuous circles across the paper.

When splattering, you may want to use a stencil to protect any parts of the paper you do not want covered with paint.

Splattering is one technique that you should definitely practice, on both wet and dry paper, until you know exactly how much paint should be in

CLOSE-UP ON OTHER TECHNIQUES FOR APPLYING PAINT

Splattering: You can splatter on paint with your flat wash brush by snapping your wrist just above the paper or by tapping the brush against your finger.

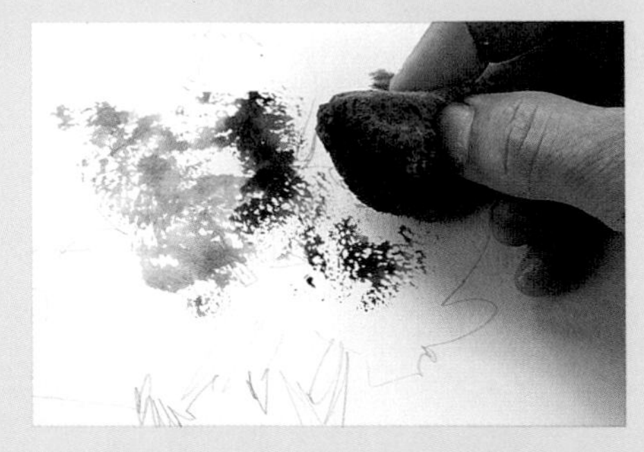

Using a sponge: You can also dab on paint with a cosmetic sponge for an open, lacy effect. **Using a toothbrush:** By running your finger over a toothbrush, held close to the paper, you can spray off fine dots of color.

your brush, how wet it should be, and how much "snap" to put in your wrist.

Using a Toothbrush

Paint can be sprayed on with a toothbrush, which is especially useful for adding just a bit more color to a wet area without making a brush mark. To spray on paint, load an old toothbrush with paint, hold the brush close to the paper, and run your fingernail over the bristles. The paint should fly off in fairly fine, evenly spaced dots, which will blend in smoothly with the wet surface.

Using a Sponge

Color can also be applied with a cosmetic sponge. The sponge creates a texture quite different from anything that can be achieved with a brush.

To use a sponge, dip it first in water and then squeeze out the water so the sponge is barely damp. Press the sponge into watercolor paint and then to the paper. The random ridges and holes of the sponge will leave a lacy, open, textured impression on the paper.

Once you have applied colors, regardless of how you applied them, a number of other techniques can be used to add even more interest and variety to the paint on the paper.

Salt

One technique I frequently use calls for the sprinkling of salt directly into wet paint. The salt absorbs water and pigment from the still-wet paint, creating randomly spaced "blossoms" within the previously applied colors. The size and type of blossoms vary, depending on the wetness of the paint.

You can sprinkle salt directly from a salt shaker, or you can take a pinch between your thumb and forefinger and drop it onto the paper. Use only a few grains, no more than 12 to 15 per square inch. After applying the salt, let the paint dry naturally, Do not speed the drying with a hair dryer because the salt needs time to absorb the wet paint. Once the paint is completely dry, you can brush off the grains of salt.

Blending and Softening Colors

When I want to blend and soften still-wet colors on the paper, I use several techniques with plain water.

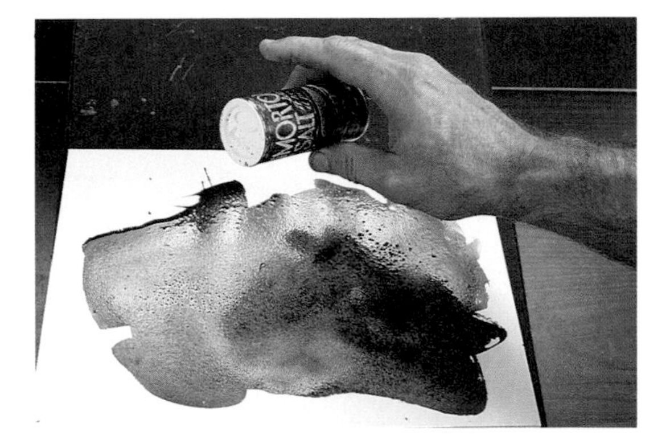

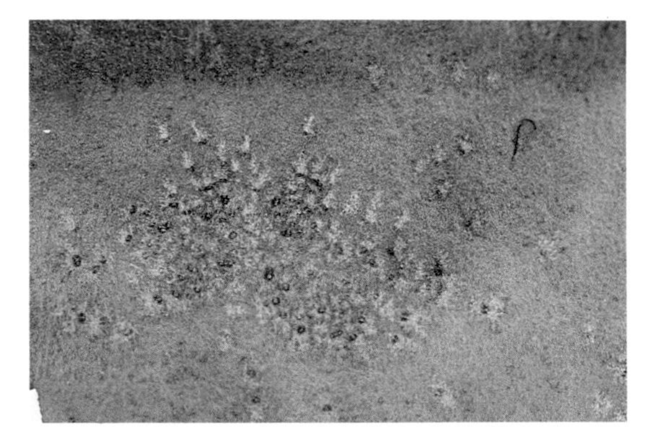

Salt can be sprinkled on still-wet paint to produce small random "blossoms" in the paint as the grains absorb water and pigment.

One way to apply water is very gently with a pump-spray bottle, using a few short, slow pumps, to spray out a few drops of water. If sprayed along the edge of a color, the drops cause the paint to run and spread out in an even more interesting shape. If sprayed in the middle of a wet color, the drops of water push out some paint and lighten the spots where they land.

The edge of a still-wet color can also be softened by being stroked with a brush that is wet with clean water.

A very special technique for applying and blending colors is found in two of the paintings in this book: *Autumn House* and *Harbor Sunrise.* This technique produces an overall soft, subtly blended background, ranging from almost pure yellow in the middle, fading into orange, then into red, then into purple, and finally into blue at the outside edge.

The photographs on the following page, taken with the *Autumn House* painting, illustrate this technique. The technique is basically the same for *Harbor Sunrise.* Do study the pictures closely, read the captions, and then practice this technique before using it in a painting.

Lightening and Removing Colors

I also have several techniques for removing both wet and dry paint that I use when I want to lighten an area, to create sun rays and other streaks of light, to scratch in forms, or just to create sparkling highlights randomly throughout a painting.

When the paint is still wet, I use a facial tissue or a terry towel to blot up excess color; I also use the tissue or towel to soften and blur still-wet edges.

Lines and small shapes, such as tree trunks and branches, in still-wet (although almost-dry) paint can be scratched in with the handle end of a brush, the point of a palette knife, or even a fingernail. Some of the tree trunks in *Autumn Walk* were made with this scratching-in technique.

It is also possible to remove dry paint using any one of several different methods.

An electric eraser or an ink eraser can be used to remove small dots to make highlights, electric lights, or reflections by exposing the white watercolor

When you are spraying on dots of water with a pump spray, use short, slow pumps to produce the small, scattered spray pattern shown here.

CLOSE-UP ON TECHNIQUE FOR BLENDED BACKGROUND

1

2

3

4

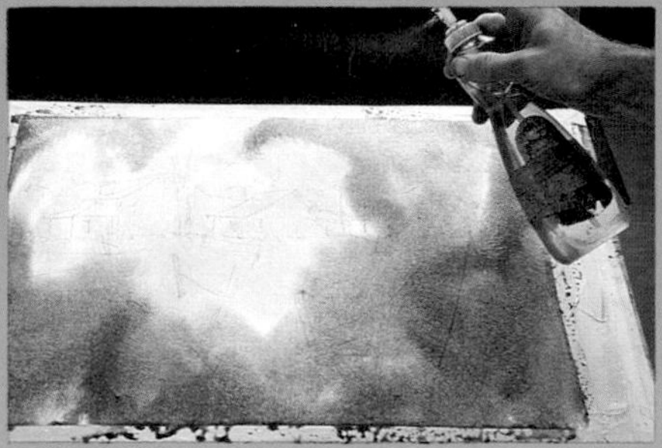

5

6

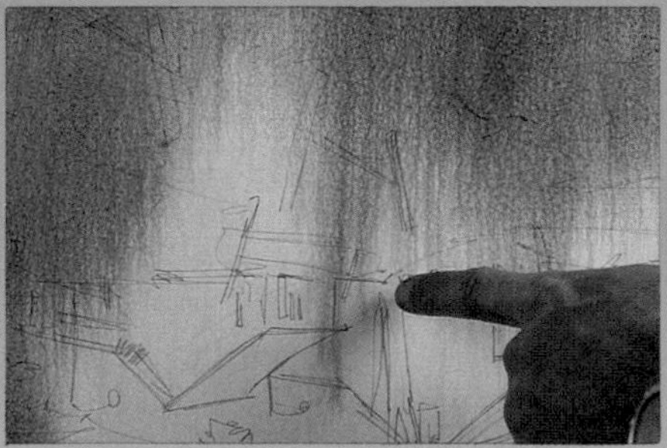

7

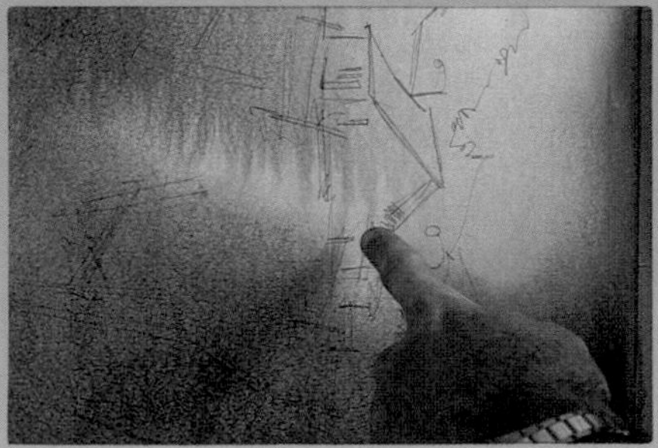

8

9

10

This technique is the basic one I used for the background and first stage of *Autumn House*. It produces a very gradual change in color from the center to the edge. I used the same technique for *Harbor Sunrise*, only with less blue.

1: Spray the entire surface of the paper with an even film of water. **2:** Apply Lemon Yellow with a large round wash brush. **3:** Spread Speedball Red around and slightly overlapping the Lemon Yellow. **4:** Spread Cerulean Blue around and slightly overlapping the Speedball Red. **5:** Spray the paper again with water to start the blending. **6:** Wipe up puddles from around the outside. **7:** Lift the painting on end, wait a few seconds for the paint to flow, and then turn. **8:** Turn again. **9:** Turn again. (If the colors don't seem to be blending enough, rewet them by spraying with a little more water.) **10:** Notice how the three colors have run and blended together. When you are satisfied with the blending (you may want to spray on a little more color with a toothbrush and repeat the turning procedure) lay the painting flat to stop the blending.

CLOSE-UP ON TECHNIQUES FOR LIGHTENING AND REMOVING DRY PAINT

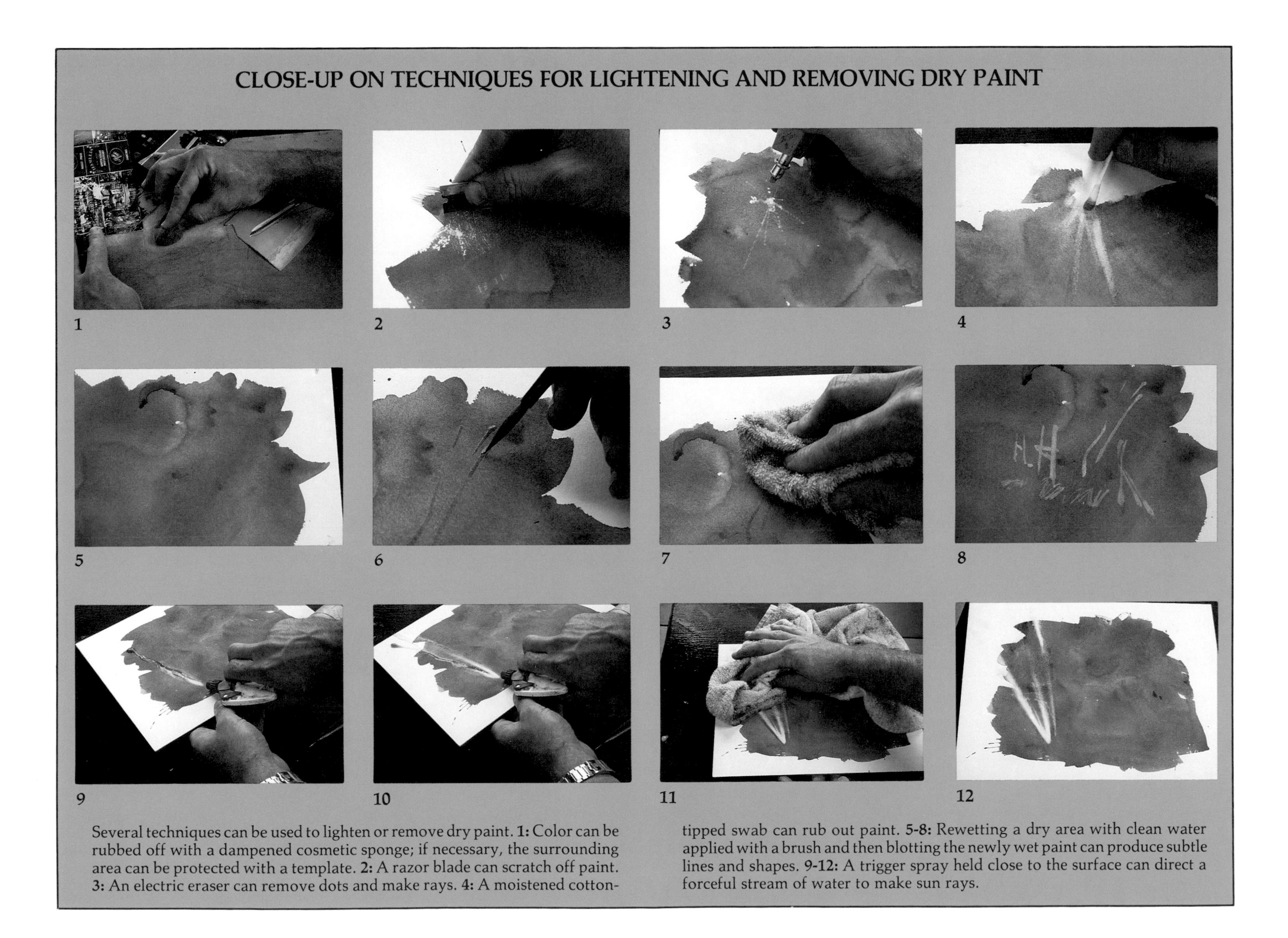

Several techniques can be used to lighten or remove dry paint. **1:** Color can be rubbed off with a dampened cosmetic sponge; if necessary, the surrounding area can be protected with a template. **2:** A razor blade can scratch off paint. **3:** An electric eraser can remove dots and make rays. **4:** A moistened cotton-tipped swab can rub out paint. **5-8:** Rewetting a dry area with clean water applied with a brush and then blotting the newly wet paint can produce subtle lines and shapes. **9-12:** A trigger spray held close to the surface can direct a forceful stream of water to make sun rays.

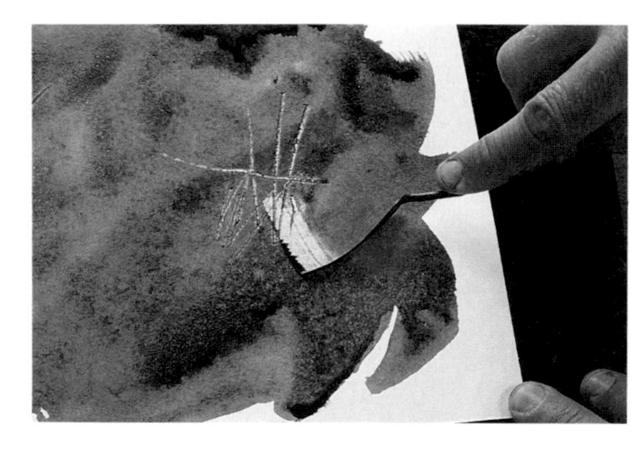

Techniques for scoring lines in still-wet paint include using the handle end of a brush and the point of a palette knife. The side of a palette knife can also be used to scrape away a patch of wet paint.

paper. The electric eraser can also be used to make sun rays streaming out from behind clouds.

A single-edged razor blade can be used to scrape off paint. Held flat against the paper, the razor blade will scrape off irregular patches of paint. The corner of the blade can be used to remove dots and specks of paint for highlights.

Other techniques for removing already-dry paint require rewetting the paint and then blotting or rubbing with a soft towel.

One way to rewet the paint is by "painting" on water with a liner brush. This technique can be used to make fine lines lighter than the surrounding area. After applying the water, the newly wet paint is blotted up with a towel or tissue.

A trigger sprayer can be used to direct a forceful stream of water against the paper. To use the sprayer, hold the nozzle (turned to the "stream" opening) very close to the paper, and squeeze the trigger hard and fast. After spraying, blot up the water and paint with a terry towel. This technique is very effective for making sun rays. Sun rays can also be made by rubbing over the paint with a moistened cotton-tipped swab. If using a swab, remember to keep turning the swab so that you are always working with clean cotton.

A dampened cosmetic sponge can be used to rub off dry paint. To protect the area around the place being rubbed with the sponge, use a template made of a nonabsorbent material, such as postcards taped together.

PROTECTING THE PAPER

A final category of watercolor techniques includes two ways for protecting watercolor paper—the use of **liquid frisket** and **stencils**—so that certain areas remain white in the finished painting or white until the final stage when they can be filled in with colors different from those applied to the surrounding area.

To use liquid frisket, take a small round brush, dip it in the frisket, and then "paint" the areas to be protected on your sketch. To have random highlights throughout such areas as tree tops and water, splatter on the frisket by tapping the brush against your finger. After applying the frisket, allow it to dry completely (it will turn a dark gray) before you begin your painting. When you want to remove the frisket, rub it off with your finger or a rubber cement pickup.

I frequently use stencils to protect an area, especially when I don't have to be too precise about the area I am protecting, such as the sky area around tree tops when I am splattering on colors, a technique that I used in *Summer Trees*, *Country Farm*, and several other paintings.

You can make a stencil out of any sheet of heavy, nonabsorbent material that will lie flat on your paper. Simply cut out or tear the ragged overall shape of the area you will be painting, position the stencil over the painting, and apply the paint. When you are finished painting remove the stencil.

COLOR VARIETY

Of all the different types of variety I like my paintings to have, I think by far the most important is **color variety.** Color variety means, to me, that the color on a sheet of watercolor paper changes constantly from top to bottom and side to side. In fact, I like to have subtle color change every two inches or even more often.

Although color variety in itself is not a technique, it does take technique to achieve. The basic technique is an almost rhythmic cycle of painting an inch or two, cleaning your brush, touching your sponge, going to your palette for a different color, mixing with water, and then painting another inch or two, cleaning your brush, touching your sponge, touching a different color, mixing with water, painting, and on and on.

Color variety applies not only to paint applied by brush strokes but also to paint applied by splattering. When you are splattering on paint for a tree, for example, splatter first with one shade of green, then with another shade of green, then with some yellow, then with some blue, as well as with any and all shades in between.

So, regardless of how you apply paint, remember to keep changing the color.

To help you get in the habit of doing so, I've developed a simple exercise, which is illustrated with photographs on pages 16 and 17. Please look at the pictures and then do the exercise yourself, following the instructions in the caption.

PLANNING A PAINTING

Many people know they want to paint but find it difficult to transfer the images in their minds onto paper. Perhaps a few words about how to plan a painting will help.

A watercolor painting begins with seeing something, either in real life or in a photograph, and then making a sketch. The sketch does not have to be precise and well defined because one of the real advantages of watercolor is that the paints and the techniques do much of the defining for you. For example, look at the forest in *Family Gathering*, in both the sketch, on page 56, and the finished painting, on page 59. In the sketch, you see just a few irregular lines where the forest will be painted; you don't see lots of trunks and branches and leaves. In the finished painting, you still don't see trunks and branches and leaves, but you know there's a deep, dark forest on the far shore because of all the varied shades of green. That impression that there is a forest was created by watercolor paints and the way they were applied, not by detailed drawing and painting, and that is why I say watercolor painting is easy.

So, when you sketch, all you have to do is to suggest shapes and forms. Keep your sketch simple, don't overwork it, and feel free to erase carefully and redo your sketch until it looks right to you.

When you plan your painting and do your sketch, you must decide on a focal point, or center of interest. Try not to place the focal point in the bull's-eye center of the paper. Instead, place the focal point slightly above or below the horizontal center and slightly to the left or right of the vertical center.

Of course, you must decide what to put in the center of interest to make it interesting. It could be small details, such as the house and clothesline in *Summer Trees* and the geese in *Family Gathering*, or it could be dramatic contrast, such as the bright light of the sun and its reflections found in *Harbor Sunrise*.

When you plan your painting, you must also think about the colors you will use. Will they be predominantly warm tones, such as those found in *Autumn House* and *Autumn Walk* or the cool tones

CLOSE-UP ON TECHNIQUES FOR PROTECTING PAPER

1

2

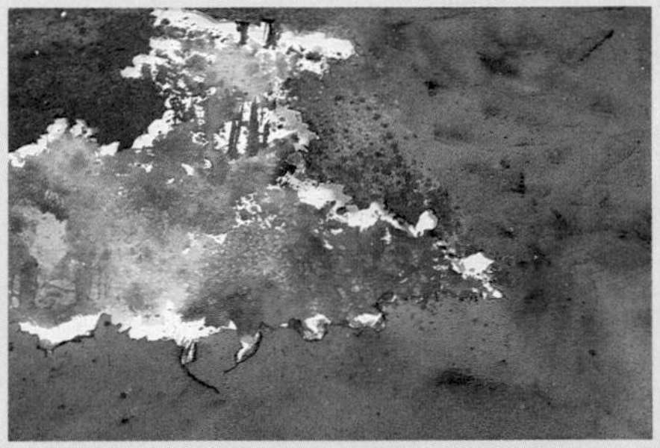

3

4

5

6

7

8

Using a stencil. After painting the first two stages of *Spring Sparkle*, I wanted to splatter on paint for the trees and foliage, while protecting the rest of the painting. I made a stencil by tearing a large irregularly shaped area, with jagged edges, out of a sheet of used watercolor paper and positioned it over the painting. After I splattered on my colors, I continued the painting.

Using liquid frisket. Apply the liquid frisket with an old round brush to the areas to be protected. In this demonstration, from *Rough Seas*, I'm applying it to the sails, and other areas to protect the paper so I do not have to worry about keeping them clean when I paint the sky around them. I've also applied the frisket to the parts of the water I want to remain white in the final painting. After painting the sky and water, I removed the frisket with a rubber cement pickup and then painted the sails and figures.

CLOSE-UP ON EXERCISE FOR COLOR VARIETY

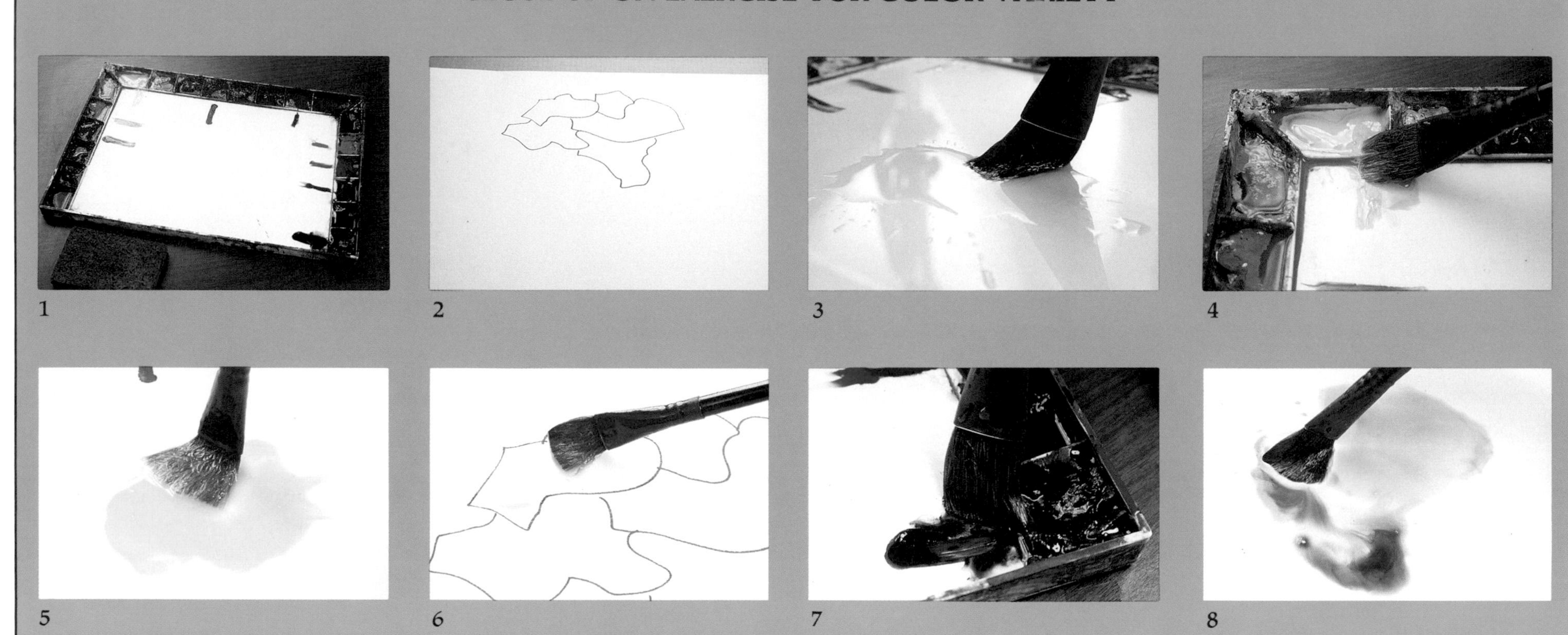

This exercise is one I frequently give to my students when I am conducting workshops. I call it the "jigsaw" exercise, and its basic purpose is to teach them about color variety and how to achieve it in their paintings. I urge you to do this exercise yourself.

Start with fresh paint and a clean palette. (The stripes of paint in this photograph are to show you the different colors. I do not usually put pure paints in the center of my palette.) **(1)** Position a sheet of clean, dry watercolor paper on a board and tilt the board at a slight angle by propping the top end up about 2 inches. Draw some free-form jigsaw shapes on the paper **(2)**. Place water in the center of your palette **(3)** and then touch your brush to paint **(4)** and swirl it around in the water to dilute the paint **(5)**. Stroke this first color in one of the jigsaw shapes **(6)**. Then clean your brush in water, touch it to a sponge, and touch your brush to a different color of watercolor paint **(7)** and make a new, clean puddle in your palette, swirl your brush to dilute the paint **(8)**. Then cover the next jigsaw shape, slightly overlapping the first jigsaw shape (which should still be wet) **(9)**. Continue this same procedure—

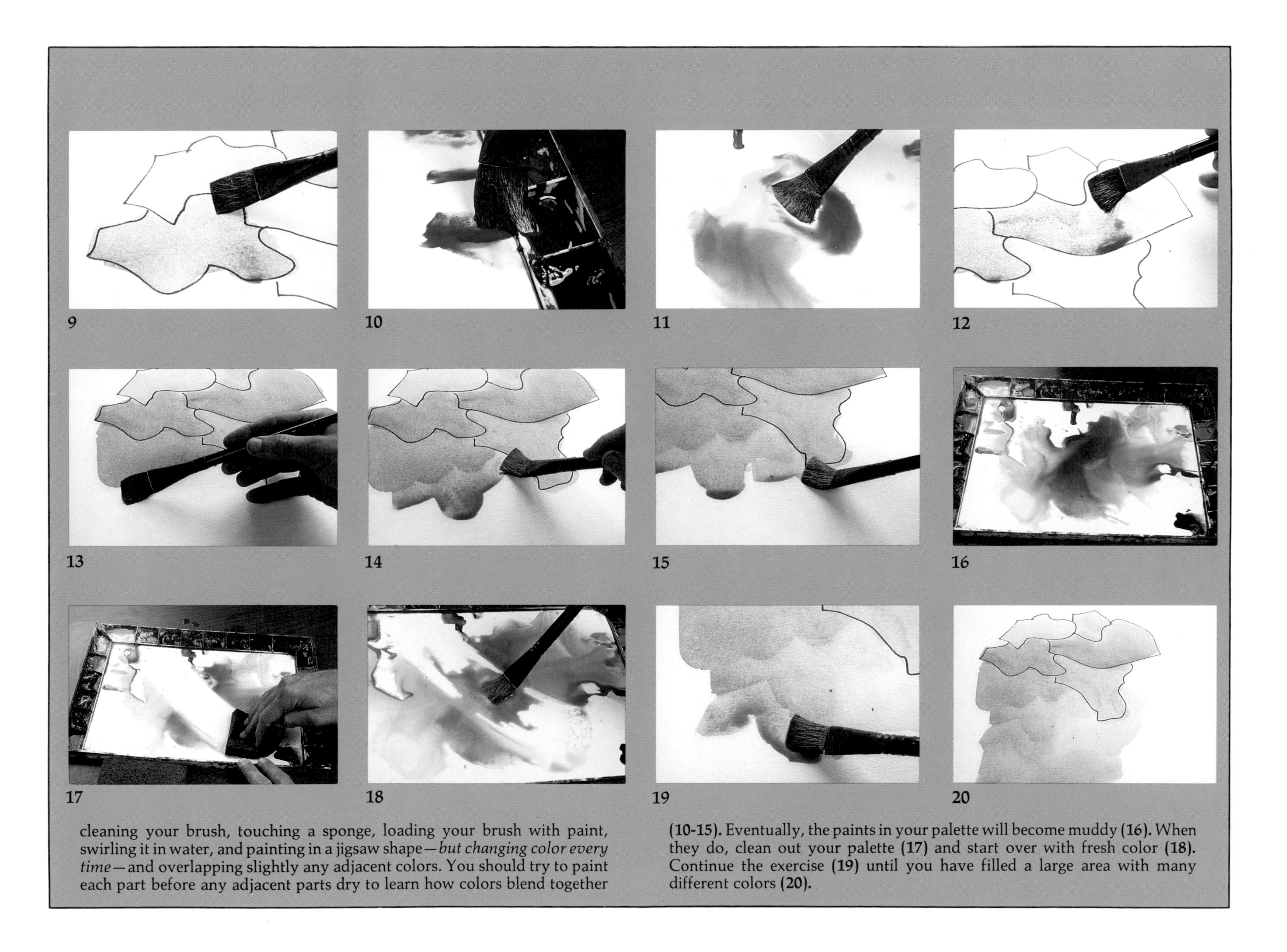

9 10 11 12 13 14 15 16 17 18 19 20

cleaning your brush, touching a sponge, loading your brush with paint, swirling it in water, and painting in a jigsaw shape—*but changing color every time*—and overlapping slightly any adjacent colors. You should try to paint each part before any adjacent parts dry to learn how colors blend together (**10-15**). Eventually, the paints in your palette will become muddy (**16**). When they do, clean out your palette (**17**) and start over with fresh color (**18**). Continue the exercise (**19**) until you have filled a large area with many different colors (**20**).

of *Rough Seas* and *Summer Trees*? I usually plan a painting with either predominantly warm or cool colors. I seldom mix them in one painting, except for a bit of contrast to add to the center of interest, as in *Vermont Village*.

Planning about color also includes planning about values—about where you will have the lights and darks and what contribution they can make to your painting.

Finally, once you are painting, don't overdo the details. Let the pure, bright colors and the simple shapes tell their own story and give the viewers of your painting a chance to embellish that story in their own imaginations.

ABOUT THIS BOOK

I hope you have read the preceding pages carefully, practiced the techniques, and experimented with your paints and brushes. If so, you're ready to start painting.

The remaining pages contain instructions for painting, and reproductions of, the thirteen paintings that I painted on my public-television series, *Magic of Watercolors*. They are paintings that I painted originally to express a mood, record a memory, and fix a time and place in my life. As you read through the instructions, please remember that their intent is not to have you copy my paintings but rather to help you understand and learn my watercolor techniques so that you can express your own moods, record your own memories, and capture a moment from your life. It is my goal to help you learn *how* to paint, not just how to do a particular painting.

And I urge you to study the reproductions of the various stages leading up to the finished painting, the finished painting itself, and the full-sized details included for most of the paintings to learn more about the subjects we have covered in this section: variety, value, color, change, contrast, focal point, and the many special techniques.

Watercolor painting has given me so much satisfaction and challenge. I am always discovering and learning something new. It is a medium that is spontaneous and full of surprises. It is, I think, the most expressive of all the painting media.

I hope you will soon discover as much pleasure in watercolor painting as I have. There is so much to paint. Start looking today at the world around you: skies, trees, hills, mountains, lakes, streams, bridges, buildings. Look at pictures in books and magazines. Take photographs. Make sketches. Think about how you can capture your impression of a scene and a mood with your watercolor paints and brushes and, then, do it! I assure you that both the experience of doing it and the results you achieve will be happy and rewarding.

THE PAINTINGS

1. *Autumn House*
2. *Summer Trees*
3. *Rough Seas*
4. *Iris*
5. *Spring Sparkle*
6. *Still Life*
7. *Harbor Sunrise*
8. *Vermont Village*
9. *Autumn Walk*
10. *Family Gathering*
11. *Rustic Wagon*
12. *Daybreak*
13. *Country Farm*

Tom Lynch

1: AUTUMN HOUSE

The soft, warm glow of this painting is easily achieved with just a few colors that flow together gently.

Here are the brushes, paints, and other supplies you'll need for *Autumn House*:

Brushes
1-inch flat wash brush
½-inch flat wash brush
No. 7 round wash brush
No. 4 fine-point round brush

Watercolor Paints
Lemon Yellow
Speedball Red
Permanent Magenta
Cobalt Blue
Burnt Sienna
Payne's Gray
Ultra Blue

Other Supplies
Pump spray bottle
Toothbrush
Postcards
Cosmetic sponge
Electric eraser or ink eraser

BEFORE YOU BEGIN PAINTING

For *Autumn House*, use a 15″ x 22″ sheet of 140-pound cold-pressed watercolor paper that has been previously soaked, stretched, and dried. On the paper, roughly sketch in the shapes of buildings, the outline of the background trees, a few fence posts and railings, the large tree in front of the house, and the yard lights.

For the first stage, the paper must be wet, so just before you begin painting, use a pump spray bottle to apply an even coat of water over the entire surface of the paper.

FIRST STAGE—BACKGROUND COLORS

The warm glow of this painting comes from the three background colors that are applied in this first stage.

In the center of your palette, spread separate puddles of Lemon Yellow and Speedball Red. With your No. 7 round wash brush, first spread the yellow over the area with the buildings. Then clean your brush and spread red around and slightly overlapping the yellow. Next clean your palette, put out some Cobalt Blue, and spread the blue around and slightly overlapping the red out to the top, bottom, and right edge of the paper.

After applying the yellow, red, and blue, spray water lightly over the entire paper and then lift and tilt the paper so that the colors flow and run together. Let the blue flow into the red, but stop before the blue reaches the yellow. By tilting the paper, you should achieve a soft blending from yellow to red

First Stage

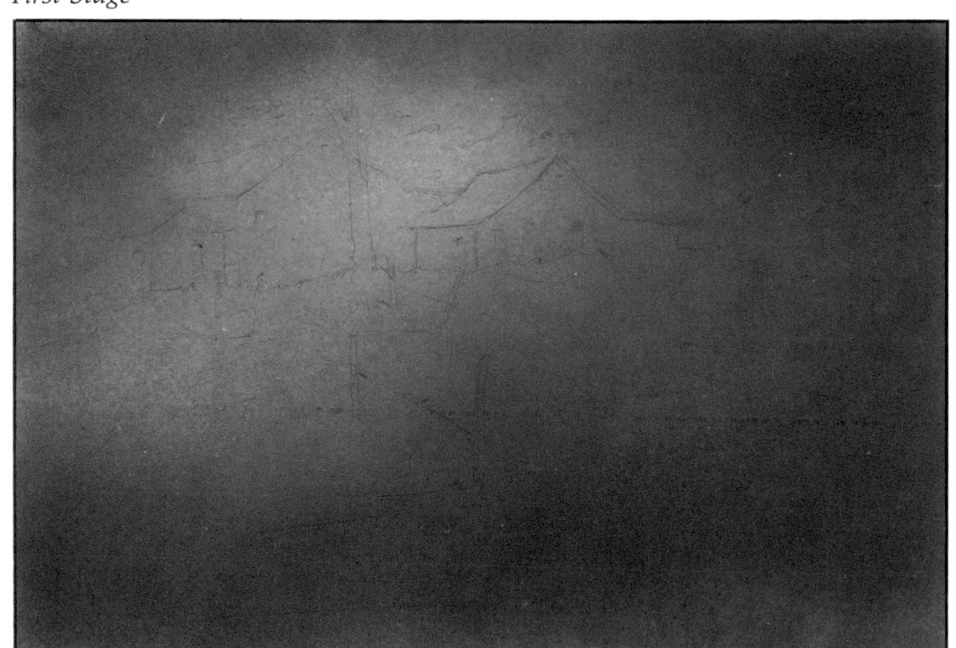

Second Stage

to blue, with some new colors of orange and violet. The colors should blend gradually without any harsh edges.

If you wish, add a little more red to the blue and yellow. Dilute some Speedball Red with water, pick it up with an old toothbrush, run your thumb over the bristles, and let spatters of red fall into the blue and yellow. Lift and tilt the painting again to blend the dots of red into the blue and yellow. Once you are satisfied with the blended background, lay the painting flat to stop the blending.

Let the painting dry naturally or dry it with a hair dryer before starting the second stage.

SECOND STAGE—DEFINING THE BUILDINGS AND TREES

For the second stage you'll need to make a template out of postcards in the shape of the roofline of the house to protect the top of the painting when you remove the paint from the side wall below the roof.

Tape the postcards together, then hold them firmly in place over the roof, and with a damp cosmetic sponge, rub off the yellow from the side wall. Keep dabbing and wiping with the sponge until you have removed enough yellow so the wall glows brightly and is almost white.

Clean your palette and make various dark red, brown, and purple mixtures with Permanent Magenta, Burnt Sienna, Cobalt Blue, and a touch of Speedball Red.

Use your 1-inch flat wash brush to paint the dark trees in the background behind the buildings. Keep changing the colors for variety. Spread and scrub on the colors and splatter on some dots of paint by tapping the brush against your finger and then spraying the dots with water to make them explode into leaves.

Define the fence on the right by filling in the areas between the rails and posts with the dark color. Switch to a large flat brush and splatter and scrub on darker colors for the shadows across the foreground, keeping in mind that the shadows near the house are more distant and thus lighter, while the shadows in the near foreground are closer and thus darker.

Let the painting dry before finishing the painting.

FINISHING THE PAINTING—ACCENTS AND HIGHLIGHTS

Use a 1-inch flat wash brush to define the roofs of the buildings with Burnt Sienna. Use Permanent Magenta and Ultra Blue for the windows. Add the shadows on the buildings with a light-value mixture of Cobalt Blue and a touch of Permanent Magenta.

Switch to a No. 4 fine-point round brush to paint the tree trunk and branches with a mixture of Ultra Blue, Speedball Red, Permanent Magenta, and Burnt Sienna. Splatter some dark colors at the top of the tree, above the roof of the house, and then spray with water to make the splatters spread out into leaves. Add a few more branches among the leaves.

Use the same dark colors and brush to paint the fence posts in the foreground and the shadows of the fence posts and tree.

For the yard lights, use an electric eraser or an ink eraser to remove all the paint and let the white paper show through. Paint the light posts with your No. 4 fine-point round brush and Payne's Gray.

Notice all the different colors and shades in this one small section of the painting. Also, see how the electric eraser removed paint to create a yard light and the suggestion of a beam of light.

Tom Lynch

2: SUMMER TREES

This scene is filled with trees. Although trees may seem difficult to do, they're really very easy, and in this painting you'll learn three different techniques for creating trees.

Here are the brushes, paints, and other supplies you'll need for *Summer Trees*:

Brushes
1-inch flat wash brush
½-inch flat wash brush
No. 4 fine-point round brush

Watercolor Paints
Payne's Gray
Cerulean Blue
Ultra Blue
Cobalt Blue
Permanent Magenta
Lemon Yellow
Yellow Ochre
Burnt Sienna

Other Supplies
Liquid frisket
Round brush
Rubber cement pickup
Pump spray bottle
Cosmetic sponge
Salt
Heavy paper for stencil

BEFORE YOU BEGIN PAINTING

For *Summer Trees*, use a 15" x 22" sheet of 140-pound cold-pressed watercolor paper that has been previously soaked, stretched, and dried. On the paper, sketch in the form for the house, the fence, and the trees and foliage in the foreground.

After completing the sketch, use your round brush to spread liquid frisket all the way around the large tree on the left to protect the sky and the house. Also splatter dots of liquid frisket randomly throughout the tops of the trees on the left so that spots of light will appear to be coming through the leaves after the frisket is removed. Also cover the fence to the right of the house with liquid frisket.

FIRST STAGE—LARGE TREES

To paint the foliage of the two large trees on the left, you'll need many shades of colors.

Put several separate puddles of water in the center of your palette and then mix many different shades of blue-greens, greens, and yellow-greens with Lemon Yellow, Payne's Gray, Ultra Blue, and Cerulean Blue. Apply the various shades with your 1-inch flat wash brush, continuously changing the colors. Spread and splatter on the different colors, working quickly to fill the area.

First Stage

Second Stage

Sprinkle the paint with salt and then splatter with Lemon Yellow and Cerulean Blue. For a final blending of colors, spray with a few dots of water.

Let the painting dry naturally or dry it with a hair dryer and then remove the liquid frisket from around the large trees before starting the second stage.

SECOND STAGE—SMALL TREES, FOREGROUND, AND BACKGROUND HILLS

For the two small trees on the right, use the same colors you used for the large trees, only dilute the colors with a little more water to make them slightly lighter.

For the small tree on the left, make a stencil by cutting or tearing a large hole with irregular edges from a sheet of heavy paper. Position the stencil so that the hole is centered over the area where you want to paint the treetop and then splatter the different colors onto the paper by shaking your flat brush. Keep changing the colors, using different blue-greens and yellow-greens.

For the small tree on the right, dampen a cosmetic sponge and pick up different greens by pressing the surface of the sponge into the various puddles of colors. Dab the sponge lightly against the paper for a lacy, leafy effect (you may want to practice on a sheet of scrap paper first), and then spray lightly with your pump spray bottle.

After completing the foliage of the small trees, use your No. 4 fine-point round brush to paint the trunks of both the large and small trees with a reddish-brown made from Burnt Sienna and Ultra Blue. Paint the trunks while the foliage is still wet so some of the greens will blend into the trunk color.

In the foreground below the trees, scrub on some Lemon Yellow and Yellow Ochre with the side of your 1-inch flat wash brush.

Paint the near foreground by scrubbing on various dark green shades with your flat brush. In several places, touch the flat end of your brush to the paper to give the appearance of tall grasses.

After painting the two bands of color in the foreground, the small trees should be dry so that you can paint the hills behind them. (If the trees are not dry, wait a few minutes until they are completely dry.)

Paint the hills with your 1-inch flat wash brush and a light-value mixture of Lemon Yellow and Cerulean Blue, with just a touch of Cobalt Blue. If you wish, add some variety to the hills with sprinkles of salt, splatters of paint, or a few drops of water.

Let the painting dry and then remove the liquid frisket from the fence before finishing the painting.

This detail, from the large tree on the left, illustrates how variety of color adds interest to a painting. Notice all the different shades of blues, greens, and yellows and how the splattering creates the impression of leaves.

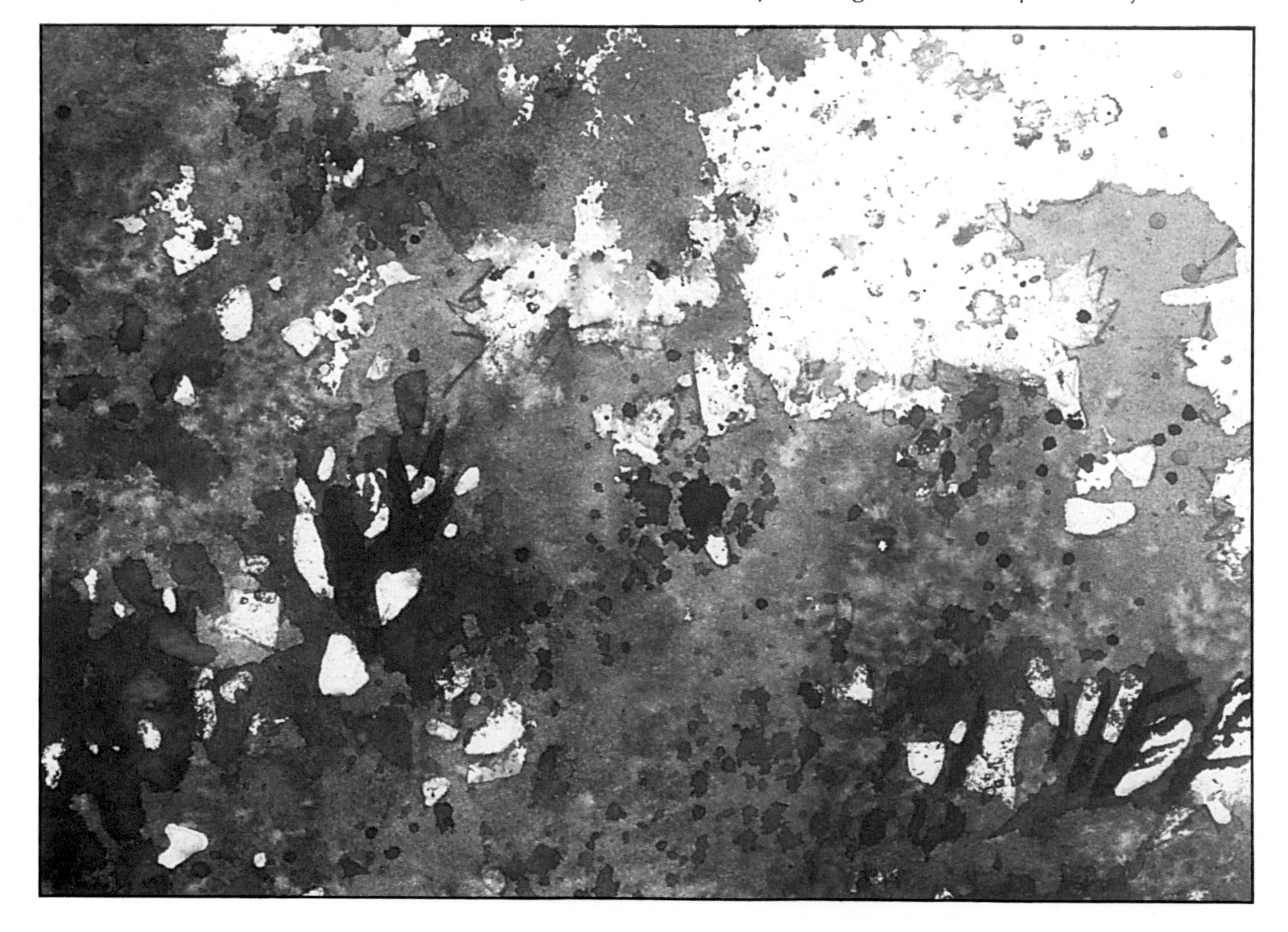

FINISHING THE PAINTING—SHADOWS AND DETAILS

Clean your palette and make a light-value shadow color with Cobalt Blue and a little Permanent Magenta.

Define the house by shadowing the second story projection and by painting the shadow of the trees on the side wall. Completely shadow the back part of the house and then apply touches of shadow to the fence.

With a dark blue-green shade (Ultra Blue, Lemon Yellow, and Payne's Gray), and your ½-inch flat wash brush, apply some deep shadows to the trunks and branches inside the large trees on the left. Use the same color to paint a window on the side of the house.

Tom Lynch
© 84

3: ROUGH SEAS

The turbulent, stormy sea and sky in this painting convey action, and the mood is heightened by the billowing sail and angle of the boat. When you paint this painting, keep thinking *action*.

Here are the brushes, paints, and other supplies you'll need for *Rough Seas*:

Brushes
1-inch flat wash brush
No. 4 fine-point round brush
No. 14 extra-long pointed lettering brush

First Stage

Watercolor Paints
Ultra Blue
Cobalt Blue
Permanent Magenta
Yellow Ochre
Lemon Yellow
Payne's Gray
Speedball Red

Other Supplies
Liquid frisket
Round brush
Rubber cement pickup
Pump spray bottle
Trigger spray bottle
Cotton-tipped swabs
Razor blade

BEFORE YOU BEGIN PAINTING

For *Rough Seas*, use a 15″ x 22″ sheet of 140-pound cold-pressed watercolor paper that has been previously soaked, stretched, and dried. On the paper, loosely sketch in the sailboat, sails, figures, and a few lines to indicate rolling clouds and choppy water.

After completing the sketch, use an old round brush to apply liquid frisket to protect the paper under the sails and figures. Also spread on liquid frisket in the center of the water underneath the front sail and throughout the water to the sides. To have sparkly highlights in the finished painting, splatter dots of liquid frisket randomly throughout the water.

FIRST STAGE—SKY AND SEA

This first stage calls for using your 1-inch flat wash brush to quickly apply four different colors—Yellow Ochre, Permanent Magenta, Cobalt Blue, and Ultra Blue—to set the mood of the sky and sea.

Start with the Yellow Ochre in the lightest part of the clouds around the tops of the sails. Splatter on the paint and use rounded, curving, scrubbing motions to suggest clouds billowing through the sky. As you move away from the tops of the sails, use some Permanent Magenta and then Cobalt Blue. Change colors frequently as you move through the sky, but leave the upper right corner unpainted, along with the narrow area behind the sails where the sky is lightest. As you move down in the sky, toward the horizon, use Ultra Blue and Permanent Magenta.

After painting the sky, paint the water. Use the same colors because the water mirrors the sky. Use wavy up-and-down motions with your 1-inch flat

Second Stage

wash brush, but leave some areas unpainted. As you move through the foreground toward the bottom of the paper, make the water slightly darker.

Complete this stage of the painting by using your pump spray bottle to spray dots of water in the sky and water to help the colors blend together.

Let the painting dry naturally or dry it with a hair dryer before starting the second stage.

SECOND STAGE—SUN RAYS

Once the sky is dry, use your trigger spray bottle to make the sun rays streaming out from behind the clouds.

Hold the nozzle of the spray bottle very close to the paper and direct several forceful sprays out from the light area at the top of the sails to the edges of the paper. The stream of water must be very strong to remove the paint.

Let the painting dry before beginning the third stage.

Third Stage

THIRD STAGE—ADDING DEFINITION

This stage heightens the form and shape of the clouds and waves by darkening them and defines the basic shape of the boat.

For the darker colors in this stage, use Ultra Blue and Permanent Magenta with a touch of Payne's Gray. Darken the clouds, especially toward the bottom, just above the horizon line, by scraping on paint with the side of your 1-inch flat wash brush and then spraying gently along the edges with your pump spray bottle for a lacy effect. If you wish, also use an almost-dry brush to scrub some more dark into the upper part of the sky.

Paint the boat with various shades made with Cobalt Blue and Permanent Magenta. Remember to vary the colors.

Darken the water, using dark Ultra Blue. Apply it with just the corner of your brush to suggest a few rolling waves to heighten the impression of action and movement.

Now *let the painting dry* and then remove all the frisket with a rubber cement pickup or by rubbing it with a towel or your finger to be ready for the last stage of the painting.

FINISHING THE PAINTING—SAILS, FIGURES, AND ACCENTS

First paint the billowing sail on the left. Start at the top, where the sail is closest to the sun and lightest. Spread on Lemon Yellow about a quarter of the way down, then some Speedball Red, followed by Cobalt Blue for the bottom part of the sail. Overlap the colors so they blend together, and carry the colors slightly over the edges of the sail into the sky.

For the sail on the right, use a touch of Lemon Yellow at the top and then various shades of Speedball Red and Permanent Magenta as you move down the sail. Leave the right edge of the sail unpainted.

After painting the sails, quickly fill in the figures with your No. 4 fine-point round brush. Use any colors that will stand out against the dark sky and define each figure's head, shirt, and pants.

Also use your fine-point round brush and dark Cobalt Blue for the boat railings, portholes, and other details.

For the rigging, use your No. 4 fine-point round brush or a No. 14 extra-long pointed lettering brush and dark Cobalt Blue. Keep the rigging lines very sketchy—they should be barely seen.

For final touches in the water, use a moistened cotton-tipped swab to soften any harsh edges where you removed the liquid frisket. To add even more sparkle to the water, use a razor blade to scrape off paint randomly throughout the stormy sea and use the corner of the razor blade to pick out highlights in the water.

4: IRIS

Iris is a dramatic and exciting painting with wonderful contrast between the dark blue-green background and the multihued pastels of the irises and leaves.

Here are the brushes, paints, and other supplies you'll need for *Iris*:

Brushes
1-inch flat wash brush
½-inch flat wash brush
2½-inch brush
No. 4 fine-point round brush

First Stage

Watercolor Paints
Payne's Gray
Ultra Blue
Cobalt Blue
Cerulean Blue
Permanent Magenta
Burnt Sienna
Lemon Yellow
Yellow Ochre

Other Supplies
Pump spray bottle
Salt
Electric eraser or ink eraser

BEFORE YOU BEGIN PAINTING

For *Iris*, use a 15″ x 22″ sheet of 140-pound cold-pressed watercolor paper that has been previously soaked, stretched, and dried. On the paper, roughly sketch in the overall form of the irises and leaves. Try to keep the composition varied and interesting. You don't have to be too precise because the background color will help to shape and define the form.

FIRST STAGE—BASE COLORS

For the first stage, you'll quickly apply a whole range of yellow, lavender, and blue tones over the area where you've sketched the basic form of the flowers and leaves.

Start by placing a small amount of water in a clean palette and spread out puddles of Lemon Yellow and Yellow Ochre, along with other puddles of Cerulean Blue, Cobalt Blue, and Ultra Blue. Add a small amount of Permanent Magenta to the Cobalt Blue.

With your 1-inch flat wash brush, pick up one of the colors and splatter the paint onto the center of the paper, over your sketch of the iris (don't worry about going outside the lines). Clean your brush and pick up a different color and splatter it over the paper. Keep changing the colors, cleaning your brush each time and keeping the colors bright and clear until you have covered the area over the flowers and leaves. However, don't apply the paint solidly. Leave some small areas of paper unpainted on one of the flowers for highlights in the finished painting. As you splatter on the different colors, they should blend softly together to create a whole new range of colors.

After applying the colors, spray lightly with a few dots of water from a pump spray and sprinkle with a little salt.

Let the painting dry naturally or dry it with a hair dryer before starting the second stage.

Second Stage

SECOND STAGE—BACKGROUND

The background paints are very strong, so first clean your palette and then add just a very small amount of water.

Mix a dark green shade with Payne's Gray and Lemon Yellow and a rich deep blue with Payne's Gray, Ultra Blue, and a touch of Permanent Magenta.

Use your 1-inch flat wash brush to spread these colors in the background around the irises and leaves. Define the outside edges of the irises and leaves by using the flat edge of your brush to make a clean line between the light colors you applied in the first stage and the dark background. Around the outside part of the background, you can use a 2½-inch brush to spread the colors and fill the area quickly.

When you have filled in the background with the dark tones, use your 1-inch flat wash brush to splatter dots of Cerulean Blue and Lemon Yellow or dots of water over the still-wet background and create some interesting variations in color.

Let the painting dry before starting the third stage.

Third Stage

THIRD STAGE—SHADOWING FLOWERS AND LEAVES; STEMS

In this stage you'll add dimension and depth to the flowers and leaves by creating lights and darks.

To create the darker colors for shading and shadowing, add more water to the background colors on your palette. Create some shadows on the large iris in the center with Cobalt Blue and a touch of Permanent Magenta.

For the shadows on the leaves, make a mixture of Payne's Gray and Lemon Yellow. As you paint this shade down the large leaf in the middle, try to keep the right edge of the leaf unpainted so the bright base colors still show.

After shadowing the leaves and flowers, let the paint dry and then paint the reddish-brown stems. On a clean spot on your palette, spread out Burnt Sienna with water and apply it with your No. 4 fine-point round brush.

When the stems are dry, use your 1-inch flat wash brush and Cobalt Blue to shadow and round the iris in the center and on the left and to make a few more shadows diagonally across the petals, leaves, and stems.

Now *let the painting dry* before finishing the painting.

FINISHING THE PAINTING—HIGHLIGHTS

Make some dark highlights on the iris in the center by using your No. 4 fine-point round brush and Cerulean Blue to make some lines on the petals.

With your 1-inch flat wash brush, add a petal to the back of the iris by touching the top of the light area with a medium-value Cerulean Blue.

To make a few light highlights on the flowers and leaves, use an electric eraser or ink eraser to remove small dots of paint and expose the paper.

For the faint tendrils coming out to the right, dip your No. 4 fine-point round brush in water, touch the brush to a sponge, and then draw the point of the brush over the dark background. Blot the newly wet color with a towel for a second and then rub hard. The dark paint should come off, leaving a light line.

Use the same technique to remove paint from any other areas you feel need light highlights.

TOM LYNCH
©84

5: SPRING SPARKLE

The sky in *Spring Sparkle* is flooded with light, and the water is sparked with glittering highlights. This bright mood is easy to achieve by leaving specific areas unpainted and letting the brilliant white of the watercolor paper show in the finished painting.

Here are the brushes, paints, and other supplies you'll need for *Spring Sparkle*:

Brushes
1-inch flat wash brush
½-inch flat wash brush

Watercolor Paints
Cerulean Blue
Cobalt Blue
Speedball Red
Permanent Magenta
Lemon Yellow
Yellow Ochre
Burnt Sienna
Ultra Blue
Payne's Gray

Other Supplies
Liquid frisket
Round brush
Rubber cement pickup
Pump spray bottle
Sheet of heavy paper for stencil
Salt
Electric eraser or ink eraser
Razor blade

BEFORE YOU BEGIN PAINTING

For *Spring Sparkle*, use a 15″ x 22″ sheet of 140-pound cold-pressed watercolor paper that has been previously soaked, stretched, and dried. On the paper, lightly sketch in the clouds, the line of the distant hills, the overall shape of the stand of trees and their trunks, and the shoreline and rocks.

After completing the sketch, use an old round brush to apply liquid frisket. Refer to the reproduction of the first stage to see how the frisket is spread throughout the water. Also splatter dots of liquid frisket randomly throughout the water and trees and spread on liquid frisket to protect the paper between the tree trunks on the far left.

FIRST STAGE—SKY AND WATER

Set up your palette by mixing Cobalt Blue with a small amount of Speedball Red and Cobalt Blue with a little Permanent Magenta.

Use your 1-inch flat wash brush to spread the different shades of blue through the sky. Scrape on

First Stage

Second Stage

the colors by pushing your brush down and turning it so that the bristles spread apart. Carry the sky colors to just above the cloud line, but leave a light edge between the sky color and the clouds. As you fill in the sky color, remember to change the colors frequently by cleaning your brush in water and then dipping it into different puddles of paint. Also remember to make interesting shapes with your brush. When you paint the sky below the cloud, lighten the colors somewhat to create the impression of depth.

After painting the sky, paint the water by spreading a wash over the entire area, using the same color mixtures and brush. Again, remember to change colors frequently and to make the water darker as you come forward to create the impression of depth.

Let the painting dry naturally or dry it with a hair dryer before starting the second stage.

SECOND STAGE—CLOUDS AND DISTANT HILLS

Paint the dark blue-gray clouds with various mixtures of Cobalt Blue, Permanent Magenta, and Burnt Sienna. Scrape in the colors with your 1-inch flat wash brush, remembering to leave the white area above the top of the cloud unpainted and to keep the overall form of the cloud irregular and interesting.

When you have finished painting the clouds, use your pump spray bottle to apply a few drops of water to the dark edges to break up the irregular line even more.

Use the same dark cloud colors for the distant hills on the far shore of the lake. Scrape on the colors, remembering to keep the top edge uneven and varied.

Complete this part of the painting by spreading on a few smooth, calm reflections of the dark clouds in the water, keeping the more-distant reflections lighter than the nearer reflections.

Let the painting dry before starting the third stage.

THIRD STAGE—TREES

Before painting the trees, you'll need to make a stencil to protect the sky and water area around the trees. For the stencil, use a large sheet of heavy paper and cut or tear out a shape approximately like the overall shape of the trees you see reproduced in the third stage. Keep the edges of the stencil irregular.

After positioning the stencil on the left side of the painting, clean your palette and mix various shades of bright yellows and greens with Lemon Yellow, Ultra Blue, and Payne's Gray.

Pick up the different colors with your 1-inch flat wash brush and shake the brush to splatter the paints onto the paper inside the stencil. Leave some areas unpainted—don't fill the area within the stencil completely. Use the edge of your brush to make some trunks and branches in the unpainted areas.

Next, sprinkle the trees with a little bit of salt and splatter with drops of Lemon Yellow, Cobalt Blue, and Cerulean Blue. After splattering, remove the stencil, and if you wish, add a few more branches at the top of the painting.

Define the shoreline beneath the trees with a dark green mixture of Lemon Yellow and Payne's Gray and use the same dark color for the rocks in the foreground.

Let the painting dry before finishing the painting.

Third Stage

FINISHING THE PAINTING—ACCENTS AND HIGHLIGHTS

After the painting is dry, remove the liquid frisket with a rubber cement pickup.

Complete the shoreline between the base of the trees and the dark green by adding a mixture of Lemon Yellow and Yellow Ochre.

Fill in the area between the tree trunks on the far left with some light Cerulean Blue and add some reflections to the water with some dark green tones.

For final touches, use an electric eraser to make rays of sunlight streaming in all directions from behind the cloud and use a razor blade to remove some small patches of paint from the water for sparkling highlights.

Tom Lynch
©84

6: STILL LIFE

There's nothing still about this painting because it's so alive with color. Although you'll use every color on your palette, this painting is easy because the shapes are quite simple and the objects are not painted individually but in large washes.

Here are the brushes, paints, and other supplies you'll need for *Still Life*:

Brushes
1-inch flat wash brush
½-inch flat wash brush
No. 4 fine-point round brush

Watercolor Paints
Payne's Gray
Ultra Blue
Cobalt Blue
Cerulean Blue
Permanent Magenta
Speedball Red
Yellow Ochre
Lemon Yellow
Burnt Sienna

First Stage

BEFORE YOU BEGIN PAINTING

Since the last stage of this painting calls for rubbing out paint with a terry towel, you may prefer to do this painting on 100-pound illustration board, which is sturdier than the standard 140-pound watercolor paper. However, with a little bit of care, you can rub out paint from watercolor paper without damaging it, so use whichever surface you can work with most comfortably.

After selecting your surface, sketch in all the major elements of the still life: the grapes, apple, orange, basket, and bottle. Remember that these are simple geometric shapes: circles for the fruit, rectangles and a curve for the basket, and straight lines for the bottle.

FIRST STAGE—BLOCKING IN THE COLORS

In this first stage you'll quickly define the basic shapes of the objects in the still life by blocking in the colors. Use your 1-inch flat wash brush for all of this stage.

Start with a clean palette and a little bit of water and put out most of the colors: Cerulean Blue, Permanent Magenta, Yellow Ochre, Lemon Yellow, and Speedball Red.

First paint the grapes to the left of the basket with a light green shade made from Cerulean Blue and Lemon Yellow. As you paint the grapes, leave some of the white surface unpainted.

The apple is next. Use various tones of red, orange, and purple, made with Lemon Yellow, Speedball Red, Permanent Magenta, and Cobalt Blue. Remember to keep changing the colors and to keep the colors clean and bright. Also, leave a few small patches unpainted for highlights in the finished painting.

After painting the apple, paint the orange. Use the same reds you used for the apple, only add a bit more Lemon Yellow to them.

By this point, the colors on your palette may have become muddy. If so, clean your palette and put out fresh colors.

On the right side of the basket, paint the purple grapes with Cobalt Blue, Ultra Blue, and Permanent Magenta. For the grape leaves use some yellowish-green tones made with Lemon Yellow and Cerulean Blue.

Paint the bottle with various mixtures of Lemon Yellow, Payne's Gray, Cobalt Blue, and Ultra Blue.

For the basket, use Yellow Ochre and Burnt Sienna, and then add some darker purplish tones made with Cobalt Blue, Permanent Magenta, and Burnt Sienna.

Complete the first stage by blocking in the basic color for the tablecloth. Use Yellow Ochre for the far side and then gradually darken the color as you come forward by first adding Burnt Sienna and then Permanent Magenta.

Let the painting dry naturally or dry it with a hair dryer before finishing the painting.

FINISHING THE PAINTING—SHADOWS, HIGHLIGHTS, AND BACKGROUND

For most of the second stage you'll be defining and giving dimension to the objects in the still life by adding shadows. Because you'll be applying paint in small areas, switch to your ½-inch flat wash brush for the first part of this stage.

To make the shadow color, mix Cobalt Blue and a little Permanent Magenta with water on your palette. When you apply this shadow color, keep the division between light and shadow irregular.

Apply the shadow color first to the green grapes. Shadow some of the grapes completely, others only partially, and leave some grapes unshadowed. Soften the edge of the shadows by touching with a clean, damp brush to blend the shadow color into the color underneath.

For the apple, apply the shadow color to the dark side, but leave the edge of the shadow where it meets the light irregular.

Shadow the orange next, but apply less shadow than to the apple, and shadow the bottle.

For the basket, apply the shadow with a few vertical and horizontal strokes to suggest the basket weave. Also shadow the underside of the handle on the far side and the outside on the near side. In the open corner of the basket, apply a little dark blue made with Ultra Blue and Payne's Gray.

After applying all the shadows, you can start adding highlights to the objects in the still life by removing paint.

To remove paint, use your No. 4 fine-point round brush. Dip the brush in water and stroke the brush over the area you want to highlight. After "painting" the highlight with water, blot the area with a terry towel for a second and then firmly rub it over the wet area to remove the paint. The harder you rub, the more paint will be removed.

Make highlights using this technique on the green and purple grapes, the basket, and the tablecloth. On the bottle, make a squiggly line of water with your brush so that the resulting highlight suggests the way glass reflects light.

After making the highlights, fill in the dark blue background. Use your 1-inch flat wash brush and mixture of Ultra Blue and Payne's Gray. On the right, keep the mixture fairly dark and shape and define the leaves above the purple grapes by cutting in with the flat edge of your brush. Also leave a thin strip unpainted above the bottle.

As you move to the left of the background, gradually lighten the blue by adding more water to the paints on your palette.

As a final touch to the scene, use some light-value background color to shadow and define the edge of the tablecloth where it hangs over the edge of the table.

Carefully look at the apple and the different colors with which it was painted. It is not solid red; it is, instead, various shades of orange, bright red, and purple. These variations help to shape and define the apple and, perhaps most important, make it interesting. In this detail, also notice how the background changes from a deep value, on the right behind the basket handle, to a lighter value on the left.

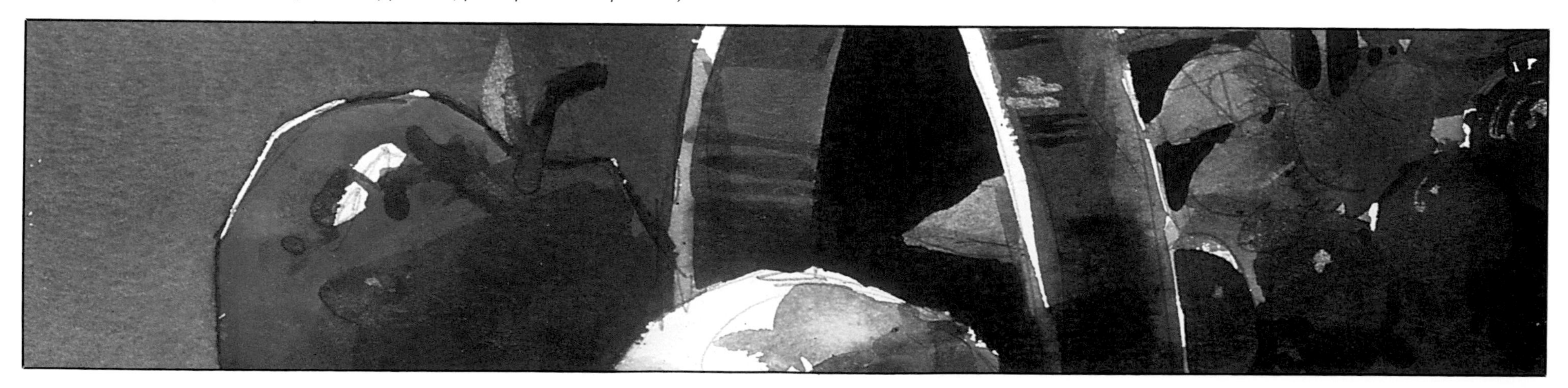

Tom Lynch
©84

7: HARBOR SUNRISE

In *Harbor Sunrise*, the warm yellows and reds from the sun are pushing back the cool blues of the night, and you can almost feel the temperature rising when you look at the painting.

Here are the brushes, paints, and other supplies you'll need for *Harbor Sunrise*:

Brushes
1-inch flat wash brush
½-inch flat wash brush
No. 7 round wash brush
No. 4 fine-point round brush
No. 14 extra-long pointed lettering brush

Watercolor Paints
Lemon Yellow
Speedball Red
Cobalt Blue
Permanent Magenta
Ultra Blue
Burnt Sienna

Other Supplies
Liquid frisket
Round brush
Rubber cement pickup
Pump spray bottle
Toothbrush
Razor blade

BEFORE YOU BEGIN PAINTING

For *Harbor Sunrise*, use a 15″ x 22″ sheet of 140-pound cold-pressed watercolor paper that has been previously soaked, stretched, and dried. On the paper, lightly sketch in the shapes of the boats, their masts, and their reflections in the water. Also sketch in a circle for the sun just above the horizon line, some leaves in the upper right corner, and a diagonal line for the pier in the lower left foreground.

After completing your sketch, use an old round brush and liquid frisket to protect the paper underneath the sun and underneath the water below the sun, as shown by the gray areas in the reproduction of the first stage. Also splatter dots of liquid frisket randomly throughout the water.

FIRST STAGE—BACKGROUND COLORS

Begin the first stage by using your pump spray to wet the paper with a heavy mist of water.

Then put separate puddles of pure Lemon Yellow, pure Speedball Red, and pure Cobalt Blue, each slightly diluted with water, in your palette. Completely saturate your No. 7 round wash brush with Lemon Yellow and quickly spread and scrub on the

First Stage

Second Stage

yellow in a fairly wide band across the middle of the paper out to both sides from the sun. Then clean your brush (or use a second large round brush if you have one) and fill it with Speedball Red and spread and scrub on the red above and below the yellow, slightly overlapping the yellow. Clean your brush again and spread Cobalt Blue around the top, bottom, and right side of the paper, irregularly overlapping the red.

The next step is to blend the colors together. First, use a terry towel to wipe up any puddles of water from around the edge of the board, and then lightly spray the painting with water to help the colors flow together. After spraying, pick up the painting, holding it at a right angle to the floor, and turn it around so the colors flow from the outside in toward the center. In this way, the blue flows into the red and the red into the yellow so that the three colors soften and blend together into gentle gradations of tones.

If you feel the colors need to be a little stronger, use a toothbrush to flick spots of more diluted red, blue, or yellow onto the painting, spray with more water, and then lift and turn the painting again.

When you are satisfied with the background tones, lay the painting flat to stop the blending, and then *let the painting dry* naturally or dry it with a hair dryer before starting the second stage.

SECOND STAGE—BOATS, REFLECTIONS, LEAVES, AND PIER

In this stage of the painting, it is especially important to remember that objects in the far background should be painted with light-value colors (dilute the paint with quite a bit of water); objects in the midground should be of medium-value colors (dilute the paints with less water); and objects in the foreground should be of dark-value colors (dilute the paints with just a little water).

Keeping in mind those guidelines, paint the boats, the leaves, and the dock. For the boats, the basic mixture is Cobalt Blue, Permanent Magenta, and Burnt Sienna. Use a light value of this mixture for the background boats, a medium value for the midground boats, and a dark value for the two large foreground boats. For the leaves and pier in the foreground, use a dark-value mixture of Ultra Blue and Speedball Red with just a touch of Burnt Sienna.

Use your ½-inch flat wash brush for the small boats in the distance and then switch to your 1-inch flat wash brush for the large boats, pier, and leaves.

Remember to paint the boats' masts. For the masts, use the flat end of your brush and just touch it lightly to the paper. You can also use your No. 4 fine-point round brush or a No. 14 extra-long pointed lettering brush for masts and for the rigging coming off the masts.

For reflections, use the corner of your ½-inch flat wash brush to make some smooth washes of light-value colors beneath the boats and thin, wiggly lines for the masts' reflections.

To paint the leaves in the upper right corner, touch and dab with the corner of your flat wash brush to suggest clusters of leaves of different sizes and shapes. For a few branches among the leaves, use your No. 4 fine-point round brush or a No. 14 extra-long lettering brush to pull out some of the paint from the leaves.

Now *let the painting dry* before finishing the painting.

FINISHING THE PAINTING—ACCENTS

Look at your painting carefully. For final touches you may want to add a few more long reflections to the water or possibly paint some birds along the edge of the pier.

After you have added any of these final touches, remove all the liquid frisket from the sun and water. If you feel your painting needs a few more sparkling highlights, use the corner of a razor blade to scratch out dots of paint.

The boats in this detail show how value changes with distance. The boats in the background are painted a light value; the boats in the midground are painted in a middle value; and the large boat, closest to the foreground, is painted a dark value. Notice also the brightness of the unpainted watercolor paper.

Tom Lynch
© 84

8: VERMONT VILLAGE

I discovered this village while skiing. It had all the elements of a painting, it just needed some excitement. I wanted the feeling of a fresh layer of snow having fallen and the only light to fall upon the houses huddled close together.

Here are the brushes, paints, and other supplies you'll need for *Vermont Village*:

Brushes
1-inch flat wash brush
2½-inch brush
No. 4 fine-point round brush

Watercolor Paints
Cerulean Blue
Cobalt Blue
Ultra Blue
Payne's Gray
Permanent Magenta
Burnt Sienna
Speedball Red
Lemon Yellow

Other Supplies
Pump spray bottle

BEFORE YOU BEGIN PAINTING

For *Vermont Village*, use a 15" x 22" sheet of 140-pound cold-pressed watercolor paper that has been previously soaked, stretched, and dried. On the paper, sketch in the outline of the distant tree-covered hill, the houses and trees by the houses, and a few simple lines for the snow-covered foreground.

FIRST STAGE—BACKGROUND TREES AND FOREGROUND SHADOWS

Variety is the key in this stage—variety of color, strokes, and value.

Use your 1-inch flat wash brush to spread puddles of Cobalt Blue, Ultra Blue, and water in the center of your palette. To the blues, add Payne's Gray and a little Permanent Magenta and Burnt Sienna.

Brush these various blues up into the background, creating the distant hills and trees. Dab on tree branches with the end of your brush. For a variety of trees, use the edge of your brush and scrub the

First Stage

Second Stage

color into the paper. Then change your stroke to a circular motion, followed by a side-to-side scraping of paint. Add mixtures of blue below the trees you painted, repeating the different brush strokes you used for the trees, and splatter on paint by shaking your brush. Add some interest to the edge of the tree line with a few short sprays of water from your pump spray bottle.

To define the foreground, paint shadows with a very light-value mixture of Cerulean Blue and a little Speedball Red. Splatter and spread the paint below the houses to the left. Keep the area directly below the houses white. In painting the shadow accents, use more paint toward the bottom of the paper to create darker values. Scatter the color to break up the shadows. Lightly spray the foreground with water, before it dries, to form snow crystals. Splatter the snow.

Let the painting dry naturally or dry it with a hair dryer before starting the second stage.

SECOND STAGE—SKY AND BACKGROUND COLOR

The sky varies from a fairly dark value on the left to a somewhat lighter value on the right. To paint the sky use your 1-inch flat wash brush or a 2½-inch brush. With one or two strokes, cover the left third of the sky and trees with Ultra Blue. Mix Ultra Blue and some Speedball Red to paint the middle third of the sky. To complete the sky, use Cobalt Blue and a little Speedball Red on the right third. With this last mixture, go over the entire background of the painting above the houses and line of the hill in the foreground. Use your 1-inch flat wash brush when you paint around the houses.

Let the painting dry before finishing the painting.

FINISHING THE PAINTING—HOUSES AND TREES

Start with a fresh palette and clean water. Use your 1-inch flat wash brush and bright colors to paint the center of interest, the houses. Make separate puddles of Burnt Sienna, Speedball Red, and Lemon Yellow. Block in one flat tone as you fill in each house.

Next paint the trees behind the houses. Combine Payne's Gray, Lemon Yellow, and Ultra Blue and scrape your brush, creating dark shapes of trees. Splatter Lemon Yellow accents in the trees by tapping the brush against your finger. Take the handle end of a No. 4 fine-point round brush and scratch out branches. Paint in more branches with your No. 4 brush.

Switch to your 1-inch flat wash brush and Cobalt Blue and paint the shadows in the foreground and on a few of the roofs. Spray the snow with gentle dots of water.

Now using your No. 4 brush, Cobalt Blue, and Permanent Magenta, add a few finishing touches to the houses—a door, windows, and shadows under the roofs. Dab the shadows with a towel. Complete the picture by using your No. 4 brush to paint a few weeds of Burnt Sienna and to make the long blue shadows cast by the weeds.

The brightly multicolored houses, although small, make a very effective point of interest because they contrast so dramatically with the cool tones of the rest of the painting.

Tom Lynch
©84

Tom Lynch
©84

9: AUTUMN WALK

This painting is a favorite of mine because it captures a season and place I love, autumn and the north woods of Wisconsin. I used the idea of opposites—the size and depth of the trees make the little girl and her dog seem even more fragile.

Here are the brushes, paints, and other supplies you'll need for *Autumn Walk*:

Brushes
1-inch flat wash brush
No. 4 fine-point round brush

Watercolor Paints
Lemon Yellow
Yellow Ochre
Burnt Sienna
Cobalt Blue
Permanent Magenta
Ultra Blue

Other Supplies
Liquid frisket
Round brush
Rubber cement pickup
Pump spray bottle

First Stage

BEFORE YOU BEGIN PAINTING

For *Autumn Walk*, because the first stage is painted entirely with a wet-into-wet technique, you will need to use a heavy sheet of watercolor paper that will absorb a great amount of water and remain wet for as long as it takes to complete the first stage. Specifically for this painting, use 200-pound cold-pressed watercolor paper.

Paper of this weight does not need to be soaked, stretched, and dried before it is used for watercolor painting, but for this particular painting, it does need to be soaked to be thoroughly saturated with water.

Before soaking the paper, however, lightly sketch in the shapes of the tree tops and trunks, the road, fence post, and the small figures of the girl and her dog. After finishing the sketch, protect the figures of the girl and dog (which you will paint in the last stage) by painting them with liquid frisket.

After the frisket has dried, and twenty to thirty minutes before you are ready to start painting, place your watercolor paper in water. After it has soaked up water, remove the sheet from water, lay it on your working surface, and blot up any puddles or pools of water with a sponge or towel. Although the paper must be very damp for the first stage, it should not be so wet that light reflects off a coat of water.

FIRST STAGE—BACKGROUND

The background in this painting is full of light, medium, and dark values of yellows, oranges, reds, and browns.

Because the paper itself is wet, you will need to use only a little water when you mix your paints on the palette, and for all of this stage you can use your 1-inch flat wash brush.

Start by painting the light values, spreading Lemon Yellow and Yellow Ochre over the trees and road. Go on to the middle values, creating interesting shapes around the trees and road with various mixtures of Yellow Ochre, Burnt Sienna, Cobalt Blue, and Permanent Magenta. Carve out sections of trees and leaves with darker values of Ultra Blue, Permanent Magenta, and Burnt Sienna. Also add these darker values to the foreground. Blend the warm, soft colors.

Use the handle end of your brush to scrape on the birch tree trunks and branches on the left. To help blend the colors even more, spray a fine mist of water out over the painting with a pump spray bottle.

Add clumps of grass along the roadside and shadows on the road with the edge of your brush and thick applications of Ultra Blue, Permanent Magenta, and Burnt Sienna.

For more definition, contrast, and separation between the trees and between the background and foreground, add touches of darker colors. The darker colors should be almost pure pigment with very little water. (They would hardly come off the brush if they were applied to dry paper.)

Add dark brown shadows to the foreground and the birch tree trunks.

When you think the background is finished and has all the softly blended colors you want, stop painting and then *let the painting dry* before finishing the painting.

FINISHING THE PAINTING—BRINGING OUT THE COLOR

To define the light-value trees, scrape on leaves with your 1-inch flat wash brush. Apply patches of color to create the feeling of being able to look through the trees.

To paint the girl and her dog, first use a rubber cement pickup or your finger to remove the liquid frisket.

Then with your No. 4 fine-point round brush, fill in a blue-green jacket on the girl. Paint the dog Burnt Sienna, using the same color for the girl's pants and hat.

Still using your No. 4 brush and a mixture of Ultra Blue, Permanent Magenta, and Burnt Sienna, darken the trunk and branches of the large oak tree on the right. Add only a few branches; do not overwork the tree with detail.

Change to a 1-inch flat wash brush and scatter shadows in the large oak tree. Soften the edges of the shadows with a brush full of clean water.

With a No. 4 fine-point round brush and the earlier mixture of Ultra Blue, Permanent Magenta, and Burnt Sienna, paint the fence and its shadow on the road.

This detail shows how tree trunks and branches look when they are scratched in with the handle end of the brush while the paint is still wet. This detail also shows something of the great range of yellows, oranges, reds, and browns in the painting.

Tom Lynch
©84

10: FAMILY GATHERING

Family Gathering, with its still water and smooth reflections, projects a feeling of a peaceful and serene summer day. And the geese protecting their goslings add nostalgia to the scene.

Here are the brushes, paints, and other supplies you'll need for *Family Gathering*:

Brushes
1-inch flat wash brush
No. 4 fine-point round brush

First Stage

Watercolor Paints
Lemon Yellow
Cerulean Blue
Cobalt Blue
Permanent Magenta
Ultra Blue
Payne's Gray
Burnt Sienna
Yellow Ochre

Other Supplies
Liquid frisket
Round brush
Rubber cement pickup
Pump spray bottle
Salt
Facial tissues

BEFORE YOU BEGIN PAINTING

For *Family Gathering*, use a 15" x 22" sheet of 140-pound cold-pressed watercolor paper that has been previously soaked, stretched, and dried. On the paper, sketch in the shoreline, the outline of the trees, the reflection of the trees in the water, the low line of bushes just above the shoreline, and suggest a few ripples and gentle waves in the water. When you sketch the geese, remember that they are composed of just a few simple shapes—ovals for the heads and bodies, connected by two basically straight lines for the neck.

After completing your sketch, use an old round brush to apply liquid frisket to protect the sky area above the trees. Also splatter dots of liquid frisket randomly through the water.

FIRST STAGE—DISTANT TREES AND WATER

On your palette, make various mixtures of Lemon Yellow and Cerulean Blue, with touches of Cobalt Blue and Permanent Magenta.

Use your 1-inch flat wash brush to spread on these various hues for the distant trees. Remember to change your colors often, and don't worry if some of the colors go over into the area on the right because these lighter colors will be covered by the darker colors you'll apply in the next stage.

After painting in the area for the distant trees, sprinkle the paint with salt and then splatter with some Cerulean Blue.

Use the same distant-tree colors for the water, only dilute them with more water so they are of a lighter value. As you move toward the bottom of the paper, darken the water with some additional Cobalt Blue and Ultra Blue and a little Permanent

Second Stage

Magenta. Leave some areas of water unpainted to create reflections of white clouds in the sky in the finished painting.

Soften the water by wetting the paint with a few short sprays with your pump spray, and also use a clean, wet brush to blend the edges of different colors.

If some of the colors look too heavy, use a facial tissue to blot up some of the colors.

Let the painting dry naturally or dry it with a hair dryer before starting the second stage.

SECOND STAGE—EVERGREENS AND REFLECTIONS

Remove most of the water from your palette and mix some dark shades with Lemon Yellow and Payne's Gray; Lemon Yellow and Ultra Blue; Ultra Blue and Permanent Magenta; and Cobalt Blue with a touch of Burnt Sienna.

Use your 1-inch flat wash brush to scrub and splatter on these various colors for the evergreens. Leave the area above the shoreline unpainted for the time being.

Notice how the forms of the geese and goslings are just barely suggested with simple lines and touches of colors. It is very important not to overwork such details in your paintings. Remember to keep them simple, or they will overwhelm the rest of the painting.

Complete the evergreens by sprinkling the paint with salt and splattering with Lemon Yellow and Cerulean Blue.

Paint the reflections of both the distant trees and the evergreens, using the same colors you used for the trees only in a slightly lighter value.

When you paint the reflection of the evergreens, keep the part of the reflection nearest the shore dark. Remember to keep changing colors when you paint the reflections. Pull some of the bottom edge of the reflection down with the corner of your flat brush or with your No. 4 fine-point round brush. Also spray the edge of the reflection with your pump spray bottle to soften and to let some more dark color run down.

Let the painting dry before finishing the painting.

FINISHING THE PAINTING—SHORELINE, GEESE, AND SKY

Once the painting is dry, remove the liquid frisket from the sky and the water with your rubber cement pickup.

Paint the shoreline on the left with a grayed mixture of Yellow Ochre and Payne's Gray. Paint the shoreline on the right with pure Yellow Ochre.

For the geese, use your No. 4 fine-point round brush. Block in the basic colors by applying the dark tones and then the light tones. Use Payne's Gray, Ultra Blue, and touches of Lemon Yellow and Permanent Magenta for the necks of the two geese. Use Cobalt Blue and Yellow Ochre for the chest of the goose on the left and a light wash of Payne's Gray and Yellow Ochre for the body of the goose on the right. Paint the beaks with Yellow Ochre.

Define the goslings with light touches of Burnt Sienna, Yellow Ochre, Cobalt Blue, and Permanent Magenta.

To paint the sky, pick up some light-value Cerulean Blue and Ultra Blue with your 1-inch flat wash brush and scrub the color into the sky area. Leave some of the paper unpainted to suggest white clouds. Spray the paint lightly to soften the edges.

Tom Lynch
©87

TOM LYNCH

11: RUSTIC WAGON

Painting is expressing, not reporting. You don't have to have all the weathered boards and rusty nails in a painting to create something that's interesting to look at. Color and contrast are the keys to this painting.

Here are the brushes, paints, and other supplies you'll need for *Rustic Wagon*:

Brushes
1-inch flat wash brush
½-inch flat wash brush
No. 4 fine-point round brush

Watercolor Paints
Lemon Yellow
Yellow Ochre
Burnt Sienna
Permanent Magenta
Cobalt Blue
Ultra Blue
Speedball Red
Payne's Gray

Other Supplies
Trigger spray bottle
Pump spray bottle

BEFORE YOU BEGIN PAINTING

For *Rustic Wagon*, use a 15" x 22" sheet of 140-pound cold-pressed watercolor paper that has been previously soaked, stretched, and dried. On the paper, roughly sketch a wagon, keeping the details to a minimum. The wagon wheels are merely curved lines that meet. If you find the wheels difficult to draw, substitute boxes supporting the wagon. The seat adds a nice touch, but it's optional. Square off the background and outline the side of the shed and its roof.

FIRST STAGE—WASH OF COLOR OVER THE WAGON AND FOREGROUND

In this stage, the light bright colors in the center are surrounded by a patchwork of darker colors. This stage calls for fresh paint, clean water and sponge, and your 1-inch flat wash brush.

Spread puddles of Lemon Yellow, Yellow Ochre, Burnt Sienna, Permanent Magenta, and Cobalt Blue in your palette. Cover the portion of the wagon in the center of the picture with Lemon Yellow. Change to other colors from the paint you've spread out, using the darker Cobalt Blue and Permanent Magenta for the outer sections. Apply horizontal and vertical strokes over the wagon as you change the color.

First Stage

Second Stage

Shake your brush for a splattering effect.

Accent the right corner of the wagon with a mixture of bright colors. If you apply a color you don't like, correct it in one of two ways: Splatter more paint by shaking your brush over the area or rub off the color with a towel.

Paint the foreground in darker colors with criss-cross strokes. For interesting effects, press your brush down on the paper and swirl your brush. Splatter the foreground.

Let the painting dry naturally or dry it with a hair dryer before starting the second stage.

Once the painting is dry, if you feel you have not achieved a warm light color in the center, use your trigger spray bottle to lift off any dry paint that is too dark. Place the bottle close to the paper and squirt a good force of water. Blot the water with a towel and then let the painting dry again.

SECOND STAGE—MIDDLE AND DARK VALUES

Clean your palette with a sponge and mix a long trail of Ultra Blue, Speedball Red, and Burnt Sienna with your 1-inch flat wash brush.

Carefully outline the dark background around the wagon and wheels. Take time to chisel or carve away this dark color. Add Payne's Gray mixed with another dark color to those areas where you want the most contrast. Blend several different colors in the background, applying the lighter mixtures farther away. Do the same carving of color for the fencelike box on top of the wagon.

Use the edge of your 1-inch flat wash brush to carve in small interesting shapes under the seat and wagon. Splatter the paint. Add dots of water in the foreground with your pump spray bottle.

Show dark contrasting color by splattering on some more paint under the wagon between the wheels and spokes.

Let the painting dry before finishing the painting.

In this detail, look particularly at the side of the wagon to see how the boards are merely suggested with a few dark lines. The wheel also is defined with just a few shadows, rather than being precisely painted. Also notice how the darkest dark and lightest light are next to each other to create a strong center of interest.

FINISHING THE PAINTING—SHADOWS AND HIGHLIGHTS

You'll want fresh lighter colors to begin this stage so clean your palette with a sponge if your paints appear to be muddy or dark. Spray water over your palette with a pump spray bottle so that the color will be even lighter. In your palette, spread a puddle of fresh paints—Cobalt Blue, Permanent Magenta, Ultra Blue, and Speedball Red—with your 1-inch flat wash brush. Apply Cobalt Blue and Permanent Magenta over the back side of the wagon but not over the wheel. With clean water on your brush, soften and blend this blue shadow toward the bright yellow center of the wagon.

Create bluish-red shadows over the seat and inside and under the wagon by picking up Ultra Blue and Speedball Red. Block in the shadows with big brush strokes to achieve a sense of depth.

Using a ½-inch flat wash brush and Ultra Blue, darken a section of the front right wheel. Just above this blue and inside the wheel, add a touch of Speedball Red. Create the same kind of contrast with the left front wheel, darkening one part of the wheel and substituting water for Speedball Red above the dark color. Fill in the vertical boards on the side of the wagon with brown and cast a dark blue shadow inside the wagon near the boards.

Switch to a No. 4 fine-point round brush for a couple of delicate accents on the side of the wagon. Paint a few thin lines and some dots to suggest boards and nails. To give dimension and perspective, curve two parallel lines along a board edge.

With a 1-inch flat wash brush, create dark shadows in a corner under the wagon. Cover the far right side of the painting by the shed, as well as the lower left corner of the painting, with light tones of blue and brown.

Tom Lynch

TOM LYNCH
©84

12: DAYBREAK

Daybreak requires very little drawing—almost all the shapes and forms are defined with the help of stencils. This painting also calls for creating textured effects in wet paint with water and salt.

Here are the brushes, paints, and other supplies you'll need for *Daybreak*:

Brushes
1-inch flat wash brush
½-inch flat wash brush
2½-inch brush
No. 4 fine-point round brush

Watercolor Paints
Lemon Yellow
Speedball Red
Permanent Magenta
Cobalt Blue
Ultra Blue
Payne's Gray
Burnt Sienna
Yellow Ochre

Other Supplies
Liquid frisket
Round brush
Rubber cement pickup
Pump spray bottle
Salt
Cotton-tipped swabs
Sheet of heavy paper for stencils
Razor blade

First Stage

BEFORE YOU BEGIN PAINTING

For *Daybreak*, use a 15″ x 22″ sheet of 140-pound cold-pressed watercolor paper that has been previously soaked, stretched, and dried. On the paper, lightly sketch in a horizon line about one-third of the way up from the bottom, the shoreline on both sides of the water, and some small, irregular rocks along the shoreline. Suggest the overall top line of the distant band of trees and the trees on the right and left, but don't be too precise because you'll be using stencils to define the shape of the far trees and near trees. Also sketch in a few tree trunks and some land on both sides.

After completing your sketch, use an old round brush to apply liquid frisket to protect the paper in the water just below the lightest part of the sky so that the water will remain white in the finished painting.

FIRST STAGE—BACKGROUND TREES AND WATER

To paint the background trees in this stage, you will need to make a stencil out of a sheet of heavy paper as wide as your painting. Tear or cut a jagged edge on the strip to help define the irregular tree line at the top, and then position the stencil on your paper.

Start by using your 1-inch flat wash brush to splatter on Lemon Yellow in the area where the light is the brightest. Then switch to your ½-inch flat wash brush and splatter on Speedball Red to both sides and below the yellow. Go back to your 1-inch flat wash brush and splatter on Cobalt Blue on both sides of the Speedball Red.

Continue splattering on paint to fill in the background trees all the way to the sides. Get darker as you move to each side, splattering with Permanent Magenta and Ultra Blue. If you wish, use a 2½-inch brush to quickly spread on paint to the sides.

Darken the area of the background just above the horizon line by using your 1-inch flat wash brush to spread various dark tones of blues, violets, and greens (Payne's Gray and Lemon Yellow). Splatter these dark tones with Lemon Yellow and a few grains of salt.

Complete the background trees by using a cotton-tipped swab to rub off diagonal streaks through the yellow to suggest light streaming from the rising sun through the trees.

Also splatter some salt at various spots in the background trees and use your pump spray bottle to dribble on some dots of water.

Next paint the water in the foreground with your 1-inch flat wash brush. Use basically the same colors you used for the background trees (it may be necessary to clean your palette and mix fresh puddles of paint). Start by applying Lemon Yellow just below the brightest part of the background trees and then add various tones of reds and blues as you move away from the yellow toward the near foreground and the sides of the water along the banks. Use the flat edge of your brush to cut in around the rocks along the banks, and spray the water with a few drops of water.

Let the painting dry naturally or dry it with a hair dryer before finishing the painting.

FINISHING THE PAINTING—TREES, REFLECTIONS, AND ROCKS

For the trees in this final stage, you'll need two stencils—a fairly small one for the stand of trees on the left and a large one for the stand of trees on the right.

For both stands of trees, splatter on various fresh, warm autumnal colors with your 1-inch flat wash brush. Start by splattering on some Speedball Red and Lemon Yellow at the tops and then, as you move down, splatter on various reds and purples made with mixtures of Speedball Red and Permanent Magenta and Permanent Magenta and Ultra Blue. Add a few splatters of Burnt Sienna. Strive for color and variety in your splattering, but remember to leave some areas unpainted so that the background trees and white paper show through for light highlights inside the trees.

Use the flat end of your brush to paint a few tree trunks and branches in the stand of trees on the left. In the stand of trees on the right, make the trunks with a dark violet mixture (Payne's Gray and Speedball Red).

After spraying the tree tops with drops of water, remove the stencils and use your No. 4 fine-point round brush to accent the trees with a few more branches and trunks.

After completing the trees, use some of the same dark colors to paint their reflections in the water. With the flat end of your 1-inch flat wash brush, cut the reflections in around the rocks and make short, squiggly lines through the water.

For the dark rocks on the left, load one corner of your 1-inch flat wash brush with Ultra Blue and the other corner with Burnt Sienna. Stroke the brush over each rock, and two colors instantly create dimension and shadow. For the lighter rocks on the right, use Cobalt Blue on one corner and Permanent Magenta on the other.

Fill in the ground underneath the trees with Yellow Ochre. Use the side of your brush and a warm reddish-brown mixture of Burnt Sienna and Permanent Magenta to make shadows and suggest blades of grass.

If you wish, as a final touch, fill the upper part of the sky with a warm pink wash, made with a light-value mixture of Speedball Red and Lemon Yellow.

Finish the painting by removing all the frisket from the water, leaving sparkling highlights reflecting the sun. Exaggerate some of the sparkle by scratching out dots of paint with the corner of a razor blade.

Notice all the variety of the light-value pinks, blues, greens, and yellows in this one small area. The streaks radiating out from a central point were made by rubbing out some of the paint with a cotton-tipped swab while the paint was still wet. You also can make the same type of streaks in dry paint by using a trigger sprayer.

Tom Lynch

13: COUNTRY FARM

The late afternoon shadows do much of the defining of the barn, house, field, fence, and road.

Here are the brushes, paints, and other supplies you will need for *Country Farm*:

Brushes
1-inch flat wash brush
½-inch flat wash brush
No. 4 fine-point round brush

Watercolor Paints
Lemon Yellow
Yellow Ochre
Speedball Red
Permanent Magenta
Burnt Sienna
Cerulean Blue
Cobalt Blue
Ultra Blue
Payne's Gray

Other Supplies
Pump spray bottle
Sheet of heavy paper for stencil
Salt

BEFORE YOU BEGIN

For *Country Farm*, use a 15" x 22" sheet of 140-pound cold-pressed watercolor paper that has been previously soaked, stretched, and dried. On the paper, sketch in the barn and the house and loosely sketch the top line of the hill in the background and the trees on the right in front of the hill. Make curving lines to indicate the road, remembering perspective and widening the road as it comes forward. Also sketch in the fence posts and rails, making the most-distant posts smallest and gradually increasing their size as you come forward.

FIRST STAGE—BARN, FIELD, TREES, AND ROAD

In this stage, you'll use your 1-inch flat wash brush to apply the base colors for almost the entire painting.

Start by spreading a light-value wash of Yellow Ochre across the top of the front of the barn. Change to Speedball Red and then pick up a little Permanent Magenta and Cobalt Blue as you move down the front and side of the barn and fill in the area to the left of the barn by adding a little Burnt Sienna. For the house, use Permanent Magenta and Cobalt Blue, using slightly more Cobalt Blue. Remember to leave the roofs of the barn and house unpainted.

Next, clean your palette and put out Lemon Yellow, Payne's Gray, and Cobalt Blue. Wash on various yellow, blue, and dark green tones for the field as shown in the reproduction of the first stage. For the trees on the right, use various light tones of Lemon Yellow, Cerulean Blue, and Cobalt Blue, alone and

First Stage

Second Stage

in combination. After painting the field and trees, spray them randomly with a few dots of water and salt and then splatter with Lemon Yellow.

Let the painting dry naturally or dry it with a hair dryer before starting the second stage.

SECOND STAGE—BACKGROUND HILLS AND SHADOWS

In the second stage, you'll paint the dark tree-covered hill in the background and start to define and shape the barn, house, field, and road with shadows.

Start the background hill on the right side. To protect the light trees in front of the hill, make a stencil with an irregular edge and position it over the light tones. The stencil will not only protect the light paint, it will also, because of its irregular edge, define the tops of the light trees.

Clean your palette and mix some dark green shades of Lemon Yellow and Payne's Gray and some dark blue shades of Ultra Blue and Payne's Gray. With your 1-inch flat brush, splatter and spread on these colors in the area above the stencil, remembering to change colors frequently, and then finish this part by splattering the dark colors with Lemon Yellow and Cerulean Blue. If you wish, also splatter with drops of water and sprinkle with salt.

Remove the stencil and then paint the rest of the background hill. As you paint around the house and barn and the fence on the left, use the flat end or corner of your brush to cut in the dark color and to define the porch. Keep the paint at the top line of the hill irregular by scraping up with the side of your brush. With the handle end of your brush, scrape some lines in the wet paint to represent wires leading from the post to the left of the barn.

After painting the background hill, paint the shadows. For the shadows on the front of the barn, use a very light-value violet made from Cobalt Blue and Permanent Magenta. Use a slightly darker-value violet for the shadows on the side of the barn and house and on the roof of the house and porch and on the floor, steps, and posts of the porch.

Add shadows to the foreground with different light-value green mixtures of Lemon Yellow and Cobalt Blue and Lemon Yellow and Ultra Blue. Splash some paint across the field to make some long shadows and splatter some shadows into the trees on the right and then spray with a few dots of water. On the road, spread on some shadow tones with wiggling lines curving forward.

After adding the shadows, *let the painting dry.*

FINISHING THE PAINTING—ADDING DEFINITION AND ACCENTS

By adding a few more shadows and lights and darks to the barn and painting such accents as doors, windows, fence posts, bushes, and trees, you'll finish the painting.

To add more shadows to the barn, use various values of a mixture of Cobalt Blue and Permanent Magenta. Spread the shadows across the front of the barn and under the roof and across the barn roof and down the side of the barn. For the shadow on the roof of the house, use a mixture of Ultra Blue and Speedball Red.

Switch to your ½-inch flat wash brush to define the doors and windows of the barn and house and to add other small details.

Use your No. 4 fine-point round brush to paint the bare trees. Use Lemon Yellow and Payne's Gray for the tree on the left and Burnt Sienna with touches of Permanent Magenta and Cobalt Blue for the tree on the right. To make the branches of the tree on the right stand out against the dark hill, rub off the wet paint with a terry towel. Also use your fine-point round brush to paint the smaller fence posts with the same colors you used for the tree.

Start defining the fence posts in the near foreground, on the left, by splattering and scraping on dark green around the posts and rails with your 1-inch flat wash brush. Pull out a few thin branches from the dark green with your fine-point round brush. Add further definition to the posts and rails with more of the reddish-brown mixture you used for the smaller posts. Don't block in the posts completely. Some of the light green should be visible between the reddish-brown and dark green. Remember to paint a few irregular shadows across the road in front of the fence.

If you wish, add a little more contrast to the barn by deepening some of the shadows, and add a few accents by painting several lines to suggest boards on the front. But remember to keep it simple.

Complete the painting by scrubbing light-value Cobalt Blue into the sky with your 1-inch flat wash brush. Leave some areas unpainted for white clouds. Lightly spray the edges of the blue with water to create even more varied shapes and shades of blue.

Country Farm *illustrates the importance of values (lights and darks) in defining objects. Notice how the value change between the light side of the barn and shadow side gives depth and dimension to the barn. The same type of value change also defines the roof and wall of the house. Also, as with* Rustic Wagon, *notice how structural details (boards, windows, doors) are just barely and very simply suggested.*

Tom Lynch

LEARNING MORE ABOUT AND ENJOYING WATERCOLOR PAINTING

If you enjoy watercolor painting, either as an artist or a collector, you will also be interested in Tom Lynch's workshops, reproductions, and videocassettes.

WORKSHOPS

Tom Lynch travels extensively throughout the country, lecturing and conducting workshops on watercolor painting. Workshops are available either for beginners or for intermediate/advanced painters. The lectures and workshop classes give you a chance to talk to the artist and work individually with him on your painting techniques.

For information about upcoming workshops or how to arrange for a workshop in your area, send a self-addressed, stamped envelope to:

Tom Lynch
Department K
P.O. Box 1418
Arlington Heights, Illinois 60006

REPRODUCTIONS

More than two dozen of Tom Lynch's watercolor paintings have been reproduced as fine-art prints suitable for framing. Among those reproductions are the paintings on the inside front and back covers of this book, as well as several of the paintings featured in this book, including *Family Gathering, Harbor Sunrise, Autumn Walk,* and *Rough Seas.*

For information about these prints, as well as about Lynch's materials and supplies for watercolor painting, mail a self-addressed, stamped envelope to Tom Lynch at the above address.

VIDEOCASSETTES

You can paint along with Tom Lynch, at your own pace, in your own home, whenever you wish, with the *Tom Lynch Watercolor Workshop* videocassettes. Two 60-minute cassettes, *Introduction* and *Intermediate,* feature the artist explaining his watercolor painting techniques in detail and offering step-by-step instructions in creating a painting.

In *Introduction,* you'll learn tips on how to sketch, how to plan the center of interest, how lights and darks work to help a painting, and how the right color mat draws the viewer into a painting. The painting featured in this videocassette is of a summer day in the country—a house and barn on a hill. Then, for those "who are brave and challenge themselves," Lynch shows the viewer how to transform that cool summer day into a dramatic evening scene.

The *Intermediate* lesson builds on the fundamentals covered in the *Introduction* videocassette, the series, and this book. Lynch demonstrates how splattering, spraying, and salt create interesting textures and mood. The artist also shows different ways to do reflections and edges in reflections. The painting—a sparkling stream and trees about to turn golden as autumn approaches, inspired by a visit to Oak Creek Canyon in Arizona—is a study of values and color.

The Tom Lynch videocassettes are part of the DEMOvision, The Video Art Instructor series, which presents artists giving lessons in various art techniques and media.

Through a special licensing arrangement, the Tom Lynch videocassettes are available through the KOCE-TV Foundation.

For information about ordering these videocassettes, please write to:

Videocassettes
KOCE-TV Foundation
P.O. Box 2476
Huntington Beach, California 92647

SUPPLIES FOR WATERCOLOR PAINTING

The watercolor paints Tom Lynch uses for his paintings are available both separately and in a kit, which also contains a small palette, a brush, and several presketched watercolor sheets. Also available is a special Tom Lynch watercolor palette with a large mixing area and a lid. The paints, the Tom Lynch watercolor kit, and the Tom Lynch palette are produced by Hunt Manufacturing Co. and are available at art-supply stores throughout the United States.

If you are unable to locate a store in your area that carries these supplies, please contact:

Hunt Manufacturing Co.
1405 Locust Street
Philadelphia, Pennsylvania 19102
Telephone: (215) 732-7700

ACKNOWLEDGMENTS

Many, many people have given of themselves to help shape my talent, my soul, and my heart. I cannot find the words or the ways to thank them. I hope that I too can be as generous in helping others as these very special people have been in helping me.

To my parents. Thank you for your time, your patience, your understanding, your sacrifices, and your love.

To my sisters, Sharon, Pat, and Lisa. You have shown me by your example what grace and style are all about.

To Richard Jamiolkowski. You are my agent, my representative, and my manager, but I am most grateful to call you my best friend.

To Hunt Manufacturing. I especially want to thank Don Polak, John Irwin, Kim Morsman, and Allan Karpo, who had confidence in an unknown artist.

To my teachers. John Pike, Ed Whitney, Robert E. Wood, Zoltan Szabo, Nita Engle, Irv Shapiro, William Florence, John Fredrickson, and Bob Doherty, you have given so very much. Thank you for your unselfish efforts and for sharing with me your vision and insight.

To my students. Your desire to learn has encouraged me. Much of what we did together is reflected in this book and television series.

To my KOCE-TV family. You have guided, encouraged, and supported me through the highest and lowest points of my life. The word "magic" belongs to all of you. My deepest thanks to Don Gerdts, who made it all possible. To Joan Owens and Carrol Ellerbe for their help in making the series. To Valerie Lynch Lee, who took my random thoughts and notes and came up with this, my first book. And to everyone else involved in the production of the *Magic of Watercolors* book and series. Your professionalism and teamwork were a joy to experience. My thanks to: Mary Lou Ferrante, Joann Grant, Gene Booth, Carl Glassford, Nrapendra Prasad, Valerie Avellar, Martin Lewis, Jim Rohrig, Constance Henley, Terry Otto, Wayne Getchell, Eric Anderson, Robert Holden, David Hudson, Alfred Lugo, Emmanuel Achille, Gary Metz, Walter Eby, Carolyn Dennison, John Nagel, Rhonda Redden, and Jim Mead. And a special thank you to a true friend, Roger Genereux.

To Janell, Tami, and Traci. I saved the best for last, for these three ladies come first in my life.